The MYSTERY FANcier

Volume 9, Number 5
September/October 1987

The MYSTERY FANcier

Volume 9, Number 4
September/October 1987

TABLE OF CONTENTS

MYSTERIOUSLY SPEAKING	Page 1
A.E. Martin's Pell Pelham, Spruiker Detective By William F. Deeck	Page 3
P.G. Wodehouse as Reader of Crime Stories By W.A.S. Sarjeant	Page 8
Peter Rabe's Daniel Port By George Tuttle	Page 20
Mystery Mosts By Jeff Banks	Pages 22, 31
IT'S ABOUT CRIME By Marvin Lachman	Page 23
REEL MURDERS By Walter Albert	Page 29
VERDICTS Book Reviews	Page 32
THE DOCUMENTS IN THE CASE Letters	Page 47

The Mystery Fancier
(USPS: 428-590)
is edited and published by-monthly by
Guy M. Townsend
407 Jefferson Street
Madison, IN 47250

SUBSCRIPTION RATES: Second-class mail, U.S. and Canada, $15.00 per year (6 issues); first-class mail, U.S. and Canada, $18.00; overseas surface mail, $15.00; overseas air mail, $21.00. Overseas subscribers please pay in international money order, check drawn on U.S. bank, or currency; no checks drawn on foreign banks, please.

Single copy price: $3.00
Second-Class postage paid at Madison, Indiana
Copyright 1987 by Guy M. Townsend
All rights reserved for contributors
ISSN: 0146-3160

Mysteriously Speaking ...

Late again, but what's new about that? Actually, I think I'm about to get caught up real soon now. I'm typing these editorial remarks on Christmas Eve, and I hope to get this issue printed and in the mail before year's end. The next issue, which will be the last TMF for those of you who have better things to do with twenty-five of your hard-earned dollars, really should follow within the next couple of weeks. It will contain—more accurately, it will consist mostly of--the long conclusion of Mike Nevins's serial article on Cornell Woolrich's last years. It is the kind of long article that is perfectly suited to TMF's new, longer format, but, with so many TMFers falling by the wayside at the conclusion of this volume, I felt it only fair to finish Mike's long project before they had to leave us. I appreciate full well the support these fine people have given me and TMF over the years past, and the least I can do for them is to leave no loose ends dangling.

With so many things on my plate here lately, I find that I keep pushing the less pressing matters further and further back on my desk, and in fact some problems have actually become moot because of my growing tendency to procrastinate—it's not difficult to decide whether to attend a conference on the twenty-second if you wait until the twenty-eighth to make up your mind. And, since I have no boss hovering over me, looking pointedly at the calendar as the months fly past and TMF becomes more and more delinquent, I fear that I have treated TMF (and you, its subscribers) rather badly of late. Indeed, the fact that this issue and the next will be coming out no later than they are is owing in large part to the efforts, on several levels, of that prince among princes, Bill Deeck. Besides contributing a couple of articles and umpteen reviews on virtually a moment's notice, he volunteered to type up several long articles, including Bill Sarjeant's piece on P.G. Wodehouse in the present issue and Mike's concluding Woolrich segment which will appear in 9:6.

The small-press phenomenon has begun to make its presence felt in the mystery field, providing aspiring mystery writers with more opportunities to have their wares considered and published than are to be found in the cold, cruel world of

Big Time Publishing. As a beneficiary of the phenomenon, I am naturally inclined to view small-press publications with a sympathetic eye and to follow my mother's advice of saying nothing at all if I can't say something nice. But I'm about to depart from that inclination and pan a recent release from Cliffhanger Press. I've mentioned Cliffhanger's releases before in this space, and I'll preface the remarks I'm about to make by saying that, overall, I am both pleased and impressed with the work that Cliffhanger is doing. Its releases are quality trade paperbacks, well worth the $7.95 or so that they sell for. I've no complaints to make about the books physically; production is splendid, which is not always the case in the small-press crowd. It's the editing that's beginning to get to me. Or, more accurately, the evident *lack* of editing. I've read three Cliffhanger releases in the past year or so, and in every one of them I've found myself yearning for a blue pencil and a time machine. The feeling was especially strong while I was reading *Death in a Small Southern Town*, by Robert L. McKinney. Mr. McKinney's strengths are his writing style and his imagination. His most glaring weakness, at least as evidenced by the book at hand, is his willingness to write with pretended authority about a subject of which his ignorance is virtually complete. Not only does Mr. McKinney appear to believe in telepathic communication between twins, for which there is slightly less scientific evidence than there is for the existence of the Tooth Fairy, but he also appears to believe that it is possible for fetuses in their mother's womb to see and hear (and remember vividly, several decades later) things which happen in the world into which they have not yet been born. So abysmal is Mr. McKinney's knowledge of his subject that he appears to believe that there are such things as "paternal twin[s]."

Long-time readers of this publication have previous experience of my lack of tolerance for the supernatural or the pseudo-scientific in mystery fiction. If people are so cretinous as to get their "science" out of supermarket tabloids, it's their business; but if some raisin-head uses his belief in junk science as a principal element in a novel and then mislabels the result a mystery novel, then it's my business--and yours. I don't know at whom I'm more annoyed: Mr. McKinney, for wasting his quite obvious writing talents on this kind of claptrap; or Cliffhanger Press, for letting him.

Unfortunately, in this age of unreason and newspeak it's not just first-time novelists and small-press publishers who inject irrationality in to the most rational of genres. Several years ago Ed McBain used real, live ghosts (if you will pardon the expression) in one of his 87th Precinct novels (the *last* McBain novel that I've read, by the way), and even Dick Francis--who is my favorite by far of all the people writing mysteries today--not only uses telepathy between man and horse on occasion (where are you, Clever Hans, now that I need you?), but has used telepathy between twins (fraternal twins, yet) in one of his more recent releases. Fortunately, when he used the twins in a second novel they communicated exclusively by conventional means.

A.E. Martin's Pel Pelham, Spruiker Detective

William F. Deeck

"spruik. 'To deliver a speech, as a showman.'... Presumably ex Dutch *spreken*, to speak.—Whence *spruiker*, a plausible 'spouter'; ... Hence, a platform speaker: Australian...."—Eric Partridge, *A Dictionary of Slang and Unconventional Usage*. Thus, a spruiker is the equivalent of the U.S. barker or pitchman.

Although Allen J. Hubin's bibliography lists A.E. Martin's *The Outsiders* as taking place in England, the setting is Australia, the same locale as Martin's *The Bridal Bed Murders*, somewhere on the coast of Queensland. Brisbane, perhaps? Hubin also has Linley, of no known first name and of the regular police force, as the series detective. Nonetheless, the amateur, Pel Pelham, is the primary detective in *The Outsiders* and the primary character in *The Bridal Bed Murders*.

Pelham is of uncertain age, but a good estimate might be between twenty-five and thirty. Small and dapper, he is married, with a five-year-old son.

Pelham's parentage is more than uncertain; it is unknown. Reared in an orphanage, he received obviously a minimal education. When he is referred to by a detective as "Galahad," Pelham asks a friend who also came from the orphanage what the detective meant. The friend replies: "Some police slang, I guess."

The lack of formal education does not hamper Pelham, however, in either his chosen vocations or his detection. He is a quick and usually a good thinker, as one would have to be in his chosen profession of persuader.

Pelham has had a varied career. Some of his activities in the past few years have been "the auction mart, door-to-door peddling, selling razor paste on the street, a little house-to-house phrenology, a few months with the circus." The latter, it would seem, was his first actual employment at spruiking. He also sold "prize writing paper," an activity bordering on the criminal, usually door-to-door but occasionally to crowds.

"He was city—a lurker, a fellow who lived on his wits, with no trade, no profession, relying on his imagination for bread and butter." Still, Pelham was "always careful to keep within the law. He might go close to the border, but he never stepped across. And he had his own code of morals."

The plots of the two novels are quite complex, full of rather odd coincidences that somewhat stretch credulity. But Pelham is a fascinating character, operating in a world of "freaks" that he seems to care about while ostensibly yearning for a "normal" life. It is patent, though, that he would not give up his independence and his reliance on his own wits to survive.

As *The Outsiders*, the first chronicle of Pelham's detectival activities, opens--date uncertain, but probably very near the end or shortly after World War II--he is being harassed by a policeman named Rorke who hates "freaks" and those who associate with them. This policeman also takes part in the later murder investigation, to the discomfort of all.

Pelham is also having difficulty raising the money to get his newest attraction started. He is to spruik for Henri Sappolio, the World's Champion Faster. After having set a record in France for not eating, Sappolio has moved on to Australia to try for an even more extended period of starvation--70 days. Pelham is not certain whether Sappolio's going without eating is a fake, but the enclosure in which the fasting is to be done, designed by Sappolio himself, seems to preclude any chicanery.

As Pelham deals with these problems, a name that makes many people quite nervous--Gregory--keeps popping up. The police ask Pelham to let them know of anything that might develop concerning this mysterious man. Pelham is not a nark, and he declines the offer.

Then, during a party at Sappolio's to celebrate the beginning of his fast, a young lady living in the same apartment house as Sappolio is strangled. She has, it is believed, been involved with Gregory, may have been mixed up with blackmail, and is known to most of the guests at Sappolio's party, who are: Dan Carey, a carnival man; Mickelwitz, the midget; Salvi, whose specialty is walking up ladders made up of sharp swords in his bare feet; Estelle, the armless girl; Wang, the giant Chinaman; the Professor, who does the art for Bella, the tattooed girl; and Stanton, whose face is badly marred and who handles Wang.

> Pelham arrived alone. He liked these people. He understood them. They were his friends. He had associated with them and their sort all his life, but he never brought his wife among them. His family was a thing apart. Deep down in his heart he knew that there were better things to be done than those he was doing, a better world than the one he lived in. He'd often wondered about it. It wasn't that he was ashamed of his friends or his profession, such as it was; but his family was his shrine, something for private worship.

Since the murdered young lady is Rita Maroni, daughter of Paul Maroni, the circus owner who gave Pelham his first job, and since the primary suspects are Pelham and his friends, Pelham begins his own investigation. He works it all out, but before he does there is another murder. As he says, "The dingo got another sheep in spite of me being so clever."

In *The Bridal Bed Murders*, the second and last of the Pelham chronicles, two years have passed. Although in need of employment, Pelham has just turned down an offer to be the barker for the world's fattest man—thirty-two years old and weighing forty-three stone. Pelham has sensed and observed rather strong personality clashes. To earn some money, he is preparing to sally forth in top hat and somber cutaway coat as Professor Pelham, P.P.—Peripatetic Phrenologist.

Into his life, however, comes Captain Carruthers-Carstairs, or Carstairs for short, who is being sought by a mysterious Chinaman—and when have you encountered one of them lately? To help out a neighbor, and because the Pelhams need the money, Nell, Pelham's wife, takes in the Captain as a temporary boarder. The Captain talks like most of the captains in mystery literature, but he may be putting on an act.

Among the various items Carstairs has brought back with him from his travels abroad is a Chinese bed. Upon hearing about the bed, "Somewhere inside Pel Pelham a bell was ringing. No, not ringing; tinkling, wakening sleeping showmanship." Despite the Colonel's obvious puzzlement about this attraction, Pelham persuades him to go into partnership with him in exhibiting the bed, with a story of its history that Pelham is even then proceeding to make up.

Just across the street from the Pelhams, a newly-wed young lady is murdered in another Chinese bed. Her husband, for reasons best known to him, had spent the night in a Chinese restaurant and had an alibi. While Pelham uses this murder in his publicity, he keeps a close eye on Carstairs's activities, for he suspects that the captain may be involved in the murder.

Another group that may be involved in the murder and in another murder soon to take place in Pelham's Chinese bed are the "exhibits" from the carnival at the fair grounds: Berta Fechter, the bearded lady; Siegfried, the strong man; Axel Svensk, the fat man; Anna Svensk, the fat man's wife; Elita Caravini, the tattooed lady.

Detective Linley plays a larger role in this case, but neither he nor Pelham finally identify the murderer, who is revealed quite by happenstance. Since the police have destroyed the Chinese bed searching for drugs, at the end Pelham, "resplendent in morning suit and top hat, yellow cravat, and buttonhole, his patent leather shoes shining," resumes his role of the Peripatetic Phrenologist.

FROM CONTEMPORARY REVIEWS OF *THE OUTSIDERS*:

"Only fair in interest."—Kirkus

"Interesting for its unusual background and characters, but no great shakes as detection."—*The New Republic*

"The story is notable for its sympathetic characterization of show people."—*The New York Times*

"Very difficult material well handled by the author of *Sinners Never Die*, who seems to be shaping up into a first-rate mystery writer."—*The New Yorker*

"Admirers of *Sinners Never Die*, Mr. Martin's 1944 mystery, should enjoy this one even more."--Will Cuppy

From contemporary reviews of *The Bridal Bed Murders*:

"The whole business is a strange and rather effective procedure."--James Sandoe

"A trifle long and slow, it's still a highly rewarding book, with as unusual and well-realized cast of characters (including a Bearded Lady and a superb Fat Man) as you could ask, and an odd blend of bitter naturalism and quiet humor that gives it a savor quite its own."--Anthony Boucher

"Really fine characterization plus the background makes this one noteworthy."--Lenore Glen Offord

AN A.E. MARTIN CHECKLIST:

Sinners Never Die, Simon and Schuster, 1944; Nimmo, 1947.
The Outsiders, Simon and Schuster, 1945; The Detective Book Club, 1945; Nimmo, 1948.
Death in the Limelight, Simon and Schuster, 1946; Reinhart, 1956.
The Curious Crime, Doubleday, 1952; Muller, 1953.
The Bridal Bed Murders, Simon and Schuster, 1954; Dell No. 840, no date; Reinhart, 1955, as *The Chinese Bed Mysteries*.

P.G. Wodehouse as Reader of Crime Stories

William A.S. Sarjeant

Pelham Grenville "Plum" Wodehouse (1881-1975) was one of the most productive writers of this century, as well as being arguably its greatest humorist. His creation Jeeves, the wise and paternal manservant—or, as he would prefer it, "gentleman's personal gentleman"—of Bertie Wooster, is one of the figures of fiction who has truly entered popular consciousness—though often misconsidered "the perfect butler"! Both Jeeves and Bertie have attained further eminence on television, as has another of Wooster's creations, the gentle and sempiternally bewildered Lord Emsworth of Blandings Castle. Yet these are but three among a rich array of characters tugging at the Wodehouse enthusiast's memory, from the one hundred and fifteen books, sixteen omnibus volumes,[1] and uncounted magazines in which The Master's writings are to be found.

Like most great writers, Wodehouse was also a great reader. He and his close friend William Townend, himself a prolific writer of adventure stories, were schoolboys together at Dulwich College, London. At that time, according to Townend, Wodehouse's favourite authors were James Payne, Rudyard Kipling, the humorous essayist Barry Pain, and W.S. Gilbert.[2] Townend noted also that his own "vast knowledge of the novelists of the late Victorian era" was a direct result of his early association with Wodehouse.[3]

In later years, as Wodehouse's published letters reveal, his

---

[1] This enumeration is based on the "Complete Bibliography of English and American First Editions" (pp. 137-155) in J. Connolly, *P.G. Wodehouse: An Illustrated Biography* (London: Orbis Publishing, 1979, 160 pp.). It is supplemented from my own knowledge of works published since that date.

[2] F. Donaldson, *P.G. Wodehouse: A Biography* (London: Weidenfeld and Nicholson, 1982, 399 pp.), p. 12.

[3] W. Townend, Introduction to P.G. Wodehouse, *Performing Flea: A Self-Portrait in Letters* (London: Herbert Jenkins, 1953, 224 pp.), p. 11.

reading ranged through many fields of literature. Prominent in this reading were detective and mystery novels; as Connolly expresses it, "Intrigue intrigued, and thrillers rather thrilled him."[1] Though he was also quite a passionate Shakespearean, Wodehouse noted ruefully:

> Reading the Complete Works of William Shakespeare was a thing I had been meaning to do any time these last forty years, and ... I had bought the Oxford edition for that purpose. But you know how it is. Just as you have got Hamlet and Macbeth under your belt, and are preparing to read the stuffing out of Henry the Sixth, parts one, two and three, something of Agatha Christie's catches your eye and you weaken.[2]

He was a great admirer of Agatha Christie and long in correspondence with her, treasuring her letters enough to keep them, though most others were thrown away.[3] The admiration was mutual. Christie dedicated her Hercule Poirot novel *Hallowe'en Party* (1969) to him, writing:

> *To P.G. Wodehouse*
> whose books and stories have
> brightened my life for many years.
> Also, to show my pleasure in his
> having been kind enough to tell
> me that he enjoys *my* books.[4]

Despite Wodehouse's admiration of Christie, there was one occasion at least when her writings indirectly aroused a sense of amused frustration:

> I, too, have had my troubles. In *Joy in the Morning*, Bertie speaks of himself as eating a steak and Boko is described as having fried eggs for breakfast, and Grimsdick of Jenkins is very agitated about this, because he say the English public is so touchy about food that stuff like this will probably cause an uproar. I have changed the fried egg to a sardine and cut out the steak, so I hope the situation is saved. But I was reading Agatha Christie's *The Hollow*, just now, presumably a 1946 story, and the people in it simply gorge roast duck and souffles and

---

[1] Connolly, *op. cit.*, p. 56.

[2] Quoted in Donaldson, *op. cit.*, p. 24.

[3] Donaldson, *op. cit.*, p. 341.

[4] A. Christie, *Hallowe'en Party* (London: Collins, 1969, 255 pp.).

caramel cream and so on, besides having a butler, several parlour-maids, a kitchen-maid and a cook. I must say it encouraged me to read *The Hollow* and to see that Agatha was ignoring present conditions in England.[1]

Raymond Chandler, who was a contemporary of Wodehouse at Dulwich College, was another of his enthusiasms. Writing to Townend from France in 1947, he grumbled:

> I wish I could get hold of some of Raymond Chandler's stuff. It sounds from what you say just the kind of thing I like. An occasional new book creeps through to Paris, but it is very difficult to get hold of anything except pre-war books. I have just got the new Peter Cheyney, and it makes one realize there has been a war on to look at it. It is about an inch thick and printed on a sort of brown paper and the price is nine and six. Before the war no publisher would have put out a shilling edition like that. I think the paper shortage is worse than the food shortage.[2]

Peter Cheyney is nowadays almost forgotten, but he was for a time much admired as the premier British exponent of the "hard-boiled" school of crime fiction writing. There were times when Wodehouse had reservations about its exponents, as when he wrote to Townend:

> I've just read Raymond Chandler's *Farewell, My Lovely*. It's good. But a thing I've never been able to understand is how detectives in fiction drink so much and yet remain in the hardest physical condition. And how do Peter Cheyney's detectives manage to get all that whisky in London in war-time? They must be millionaires, as I believe the stuff is at about four quid a bottle.[3]

Another great American writer seems to have come early to Wodehouse's attention, when he was himself regularly publishing stories in the *Saturday Evening Post*. In that same letter, Wodehouse asks:

> Do you ever read Rex Stout's Nero Wolfe stories? A good many of them came out in the *Saturday Evening Post*. They're good. He has rather ingeniously made

---

[1] Wodehouse, *op. cit.*, p. 144.

[2] *Ibid.*, pp. 124–125.

[3] *Ibid.*, p. 136.

his tough detective drink milk.[1]

The "tough detective" was, of course, Archie Goodwin, not Nero Wolfe himself. Though Nero could also be unexpectedly tough at times, he is not recorded as ever drinking milk!

Wodehouse's reading was certainly very wide, within and without this particular genre. Arthur Morrison, one of the earliest writers of mysteries, gained praise during a discussion of possible story plots for Townend:

> Arthur Morrison once did a very good one where a caller was shown over the house by bloke who had just murdered the owner, whose body was lying in next room. Couldn't we do something on those lines?[2]

Like most Englishmen in the twenties and thirties, Wodehouse was an avid reader of Edgar Wallace, dedicating his book *Sam the Sudden* (1925) to Wallace and receiving a reciprocal dedication in Wallace's *The Gaunt Stranger*.[3] There was a note of envy in one of Wodehouse's letters to Townend:

> Edgar Wallace, I hear, now has a Rolls Royce and also a separate car for each of the five members of his family. Also a day butler and a night butler, so that there is never a time when you can go into his house and not find buttling going on. That's the way to live![4]

However, an incident at a dinner, that might have aroused Wodehouse's resentment, instead merely provoked his lasting glee:

> Plum found himself embroiled in parties galore. One gathering in particular impressed itself upon his memory of those days. "I was seated next to an elderly woman at a dinner party given by Ethel," he recalled, "when she turned and spoke to me. 'This is a great moment for me,' she said. 'I can't tell you how proud I am. I think I have read everything you have ever written. We all love your books. My eldest son reads nothing else. And so do my grandsons. The table in their room is piled high with them. And when I go home tonight,' she added, 'and tell them that I have actually been sitting at dinner

---

[1] *Ibid.*, pp. 136–137.

[2] *Ibid.*, p. 73.

[3] Connolly, *op. cit.*, p. 56.

[4] Wodehouse, *op. cit.*, p. 39.

next to Edgar Wallace, I don't know what they will say.'" Plum didn't know what to say, either. With a look that might have struck the lady as strangely cold, he nodded his appreciation.[1]

A person whom Wodehouse both liked and admired was E. Phillips Oppenheim, once a best-selling author and considered "the great storyteller" but now almost forgotten. In a letter written in the fall of 1945, Wodehouse expressed this admiration very frankly to Townend:

> I see in the Paris *Daily Mail* that E. Phillips Oppenheim has managed to get back to his home in Guernsey by getting a lift on a yacht. He is seventy-nine, but must still be pretty fit, if he can dash about like that.
> I have always been devoted to Oppy. I saw a lot of him when I was living at La Freyere. I remember him coming to lunch one day not long after he had had a slight sunstroke, and he was taking no chances on getting another one. There was one of those Riviera trees on the terrace, a dense mass of leaves through which no ray of light could penetrate, and he sat under it with a sun helmet on his head holding a large umbrella over himself. Did you know that he used to dictate all his stuff? I found him in a gloomy mood one day. He had had the perfect secretary, who used to squeal with excitement as the story got going on the international spies and mysterious veiled women, which bucked him up enormously, and she had left to get married and in her place had come one of those tall, statuesque, frozen-faced secs who took his dictation in an aloof, revolted sort of way as if the stuff soiled the paper of her note-book. He said it discouraged him.[2]

Wodehouse and Oppenheim were good friends while neighbours on the Riviera and they played much golf together. Indeed, Oppenheim devotes four pages of his autobiography to Wodehouse's golfing exploits and considered him the longest driver among golf amateurs he had ever seen.[3]

Lord Dunsany, whose incredibly diverse literary output included some of the most succinct and memorable mysteries

---

[1] D.A. Jasen, *P.G. Wodehouse: A Portrait of a Master* (New York: Mason and Lipscomb, 1974, 294 pp.), p. 123. The story is told less fully in a footnote by Townend in Wodehouse, *op. cit.*, p. 163.

[2] Wodehouse, *op. cit.*, p. 38.

[3] E.P. Oppenheim, *The Pool of Memory* (London: Hodder and Stoughton, 1941, 300 pp.), pp. 73-76, 150.

ever penned, was a particular enthusiasm:

> To fill in the time before Edgar Wallace writes another one, I am re-reading Dunsany. I never get tired of his stories. I can always let them cool off for a month or two and then come back to them. He is the only writer I know who opens up an entirely new world to me. What a mass of perfectly wonderful stuff he has done. (All this is probably wasted on you, as I don't suppose you have read him, unless you were attracted to his stories by the fact that they used to be illustrated by S.H. Sime. He has exactly the same eerie imagination as Sime. In fact, he told me once that quite a lot of his stuff was written from Sime's pictures. They would hand him a Sime drawing of a wintry scene with a sinister-looking bird flying over it and he would brood on it for a while and come up with *The Bird of the Difficult Eye.*)
>
> His secret sorrow is that he wants to write plays and can't get them put on. I spent the afternoon with him once at his house down in Kent, and he read me three of his plays one after the other. All awfully good, but much too fantastic. One of them was about an unemployed ex-officer after the War who couldn't get a job, so he hired himself out as a watch-dog. He lived in a kennel, and the big scene was where he chased a cat up a tree and sat under it shouting abuse. I laughed heartily myself, but I could just picture the fishy, glazed eye of a manager listening to it.[1]

Highest of all, however, was ranked Sir Arthur Conan Doyle. In one of his earlier letters to Townend, Wodehouse wrote of him at length:

> Conan Doyle, a few words on the subject of. Don't you find as you age in the wood, as we both are doing, that the tragedy of life is that your early heroes lose their glamour? As a lad in the twenties you worship old whoever-it-is, the successful author, and by the time you're forty you find yourself blushing hotly at the thought that you could ever have admired the bilge he writes.
>
> Now, with Doyle, I don't have this feeling. I still revere his work as much as ever. I used to think it swell, and I still think it swell. Do you remember when we used to stand outside the bookstall at Dulwich station on the first of the month, waiting for Stanhope to open it so that we could get the new *Strand* with the latest instalment of *Rodney Stone* ... and the agony of finding that something had happened

---

[1] Wodehouse, *op. cit.*, p. 38.

to postpone the fight between Champion Harrison and Crab Wilson for another month? I would do it today if Rodney Stone was running now.

And apart from his work, I admire Doyle so much as a man. I should call him definitely a great man, and I don't imagine I'm the only one who thinks so. He was telling me once that when he was in America, he saw an advertisement in a paper: "Conan Doyle's School of Writing. Let the Conan Doyle School of Writing teach you how to sell"—or something to that effect. In other words, some blighter was using his name to swindle the public. Well, what most people in his place would have said would have been "Hullo! This looks fishy". The way he put it when telling me the story was: "I said to myself, 'Ha! There is villainy afoot'."[1]

When advising Townend on the techniques of writing, Wodehouse used Doyle's writing to furnish an effective example:

Last night I went to bed early and read your story, Peter the Greek. For the first half I thought it was the best thing you had ever done, full of action and suspense. But, honestly, as you seem to think yourself from your letter, it does drop a bit after that. Mogger (my Heaven! what names you give your characters!), whom you have established as a sinister menace, is weakened by the scene where Teame hits him. It is an error, I think, ever to have your villain manhandled by a minor character. Just imagine Moriarty socked by Doctor Watson. A villain ought to be a sort of scarcely human invulnerable figure. The reader ought to be in a constant state of panic, saying to himself: "How the devil *is* this superman to be foiled?" The only person capable of hurting him should be the hero.[2]

Yet Wodehouse's admiration of Doyle was by no means uncritical, as a letter to his stepdaughter Leonora demonstrates:

Aren't writers extraordinary. I simply gasped when Wells said that the Bulpington of Blupp was as good a character as Kipps. It meant that his critical sense was absolutely dead. The Bulpington of Blupp isn't a character at all. I felt the same when Conan Doyle used to say that the later Sherlock Holmes stories were as good as the early ones. It's a relief to me to know that I've got you to tell me if I am going

---

[1] *Ibid.*, p. 31.

[2] *Ibid.*, p. 21.

cuckoo in my work.[1]

After release from interment by the Nazis in August, 1941, Wodehouse did the most unwise thing in his amiable, innocent life by allowing himself to be persuaded to make some broadcasts from Berlin. His release had been solely on grounds of age, not from any other cause, and those broadcasts were not in the least political; rather, they were amusing and poked gentle fun at the Germans. Nevertheless, in the tense climate of the war years, it was assumed that the broadcasts had been the price of his release. Consequently, poor Wodehouse was branded as a collaborator.

Among the writers who rallied to his defence were Dorothy L. Sayers and Sax Rohmer.[2] (Rohmer and Wodehouse were later to be associated in unsuccessful attempts to subvert the extortions upon royalties of the U.S. Internal Revenue Service.)[3] Since Wodehouse was perfectly prepared to forgive writers for poor literary style, provided they told entertaining stories, it is likely enough that he read cheerfully of the exploits and frustrations of Dr. Fu Manchu; but I have found no evidence for this.

For Wodehouse's reading of Lord Peter Wimsey's adventures, the evidence is indirect but convincing. In the early pages of Wodehouse's *Uncle Dynamite* (1948), Reginald "Pongo" Twistleton is having an amiable dinner with his remarkable uncle, Frederick Altamount Cornwallis Twistleton, fifth Earl of Ickenham:

> They also touched on such topics as the weather, dogs, two-seater cars (their treatment in sickness and in health), the foreign policy of the Government, the chances of Jujube for the Goodwood Cup, and what you would do—this subject arising from Pongo's recent literary studies—if you found a dead body in your bath one morning with nothing on but pince-nez and a pair of spats.[4]

Quite evidently Wodehouse was remembering the gruesome discovery by the unfortunate Mr. Thripps, recounted in Sayers' *Whose Body?* (1923):

> The body which lay in the bath was that of a tall, stout man of about fifty. The hair, which was

---

[1] Quoted in Donaldson, *op. cit.*, p. 156.

[2] See Townend's comments in Wodehouse, *op. cit.*, pp. 110-112, and Donaldson, *op. cit.*, p. 234.

[3] Donaldson, *op. cit.*, p. 299.

[4] P.G. Wodehouse, *Uncle Dynamite* (London: Herbert Jenkins, 1948, 239 pp.), p. 18.

thick and black and naturally curly, had been cut and parted by a master hand, and exuded a faint violet perfume, perfectly recognisable in the close air of the bathroom. The features were thick, fleshy and strongly marked, with prominent dark eyes, and a long nose curving down to a heavy chin. The clean-shaven lips were full and sensual, and the dropped jaw showed teeth stained with tobacco. On the dead face the handsome pair of gold pince-nez mocked death with grotesque elegance; the fine gold chain curved over the naked breast. The legs lay stiffly stretched out side by side; the arms reposed close to the body; the fingers flexed naturally. Lord Peter lifted one arm, and looked at the hand with a little frown.

"Bit of a dandy, your visitor, what?" he murmured. "Parma violet and manicure." He bent again, slipping his hand beneath the head. The absurd eyeglasses slipped off, clattering into the bath, and the noise put the last touch to Mr. Thipps's growing nervousness.

"If you'll excuse me," he murmured, "it makes me feel quite faint, it reely does."[1]

Another line of evidence on Wodehouse's reading is furnished in *The Code of the Woosters* (1938). Bertie Wooster is reading a mystery story—"a particularly good one, full of crisp clues and meaty murders"[2]—as a distraction from the worrisome problem of locating the leather-covered notebook purloined by Stephanie Byng. He announces:

"Jeeves, I have come upon a significant passage.... It points the way and sets the feet upon the right path. I'll read it to you. The detective is speaking to his pal, and the 'they' refers to some bounders at present unidentified, who have been ransacking a girl's room, hoping to find the missing jewels. Listen attentively, Jeeves. 'They seem to have looked everywhere, my dear Postlethwaite, except in the one place where they might have expected to find something. Amateurs, Postlethwaite, rank amateurs. They never thought of the top of the cupboard, the thing any experienced crook thinks of at once, because'—note carefully what follows—'because he knows it is every woman's favourite

---

[1] D.L. Sayers, *Whose Body?* (London: Gollancz, 1923, 288 pp.), pp. 30-31.

[2] P.G. Wodehouse, *The Code of the Woosters* (London: Herbert Jenkins, 1938, 312 pp.), p. 140.

hiding place.'"[1]

Bertie's "goose-flesher" is not named in the book, but I can now identify it for Wodehousians who have wondered: E.R. Punshon's *Mystery of Mr. Jessop*, published just one year earlier. The detective in whom Bertie has such faith is Superintendent Ulyett, superior officer of Punshon's principal hero, Sergeant Bobby Owen. It is to Bobby that Ulyett grunts that the crooks had:

> "Looked nearly everywhere.... Amateurs though—complete amateurs; never thought of the top of the cupboard any experienced crook thinks of at once, because he knows it's every woman's favourite hiding place."[2]

Thus we can add E.R. Punshon to Wodehouse's reading list!

A knottier problem is presented by "Pongo" Twistleton's reading in *Uncle Dynamite*, a mystery thriller entitled *Murder in the Fog*. Now, Wodehouse strewed the titles of entirely fictional works of crime fiction throughout his novels and short stories—Usborne has listed twenty-four of them[3]—but most of those titles have a much more imaginative ring. (Typical of Wodehouse's invented "goose-fleshers" are *Inspector Biffen Views the Body*, *The Case of the Poisoned Doughnut*, *Blood on the Bannisters*, *Excuse My Gat!* and *Gore by the Gallon*.)[4] This particular title sounds genuine, somehow; moreover, the plot outline sounds pretty typical of a mystery of the 1920's or 1930's:

> In times of spiritual disturbance there is nothing like a brisk mystery thriller for taking the mind off its anxieties. Pongo's first move after parting from Sir Aylmer Bostock had been to go to his room and get his copy of *Murder in the Fog*; his second to seek some quiet spot outside the grounds, where there would be no danger of meeting the ex-Governor on his return, and soothe himself with a good read. He found such a spot at the side of the road not far from the Manor gates, and soon became absorbed.
> The treatment proved almost immediately effective. That interview with Sir Aylmer in the hall had filled him with numbing fears and rendered him

---

[1] *Ibid.*, p. 171.

[2] E.R. Punshon, *Mystery of Mr. Jessop* (New York: Hillman-Curl, 1937, 320 pp.), p. 151.

[3] R. Usborne, "Authors and Their Books," in *A Wodehouse Companion* (London: Elm Tree Books, 1981, 1698 pp.), pp. 98-100.

[4] *Idem.*

all of a twitter, but now he found his quivering ganglia getting back to mid-season form: and, unlike the heroine of the tale in which he was immersed, who had just got trapped in the underground den of one of those Faceless Fiends who cause so much annoyance, he was feeling quite tranquil....[1]

A check reveals four books that might have been on Wodehouse's reading list: Paul Thorne's *Murder in the Fog* (Penn, 1929); Elaine Hamilton's *Murder in the Fog* (Paul, 1931); Henry Leford Gales' *Murder in the Fog* (McCaulay, 1932: British title *Murder in the Mist*); and, slightly less likely, Richard Worth's *The Murder in the Fog* (Aldine, 1927). I have been able to find none of these works but, if one did indeed contain a heroine trapped in an underground den by Faceless Fiends, we can add another author to Wodehouse's reading list!

Not only did Wodehouse invent fictional titles of crime stories, but also his humorous novels several times had crime writers as principal characters. The earliest is one of his most sympathetic heroes, Ashe Marson (pseudonym "Gridley Quayle") in *Something Fresh* (1915), the first of the Blandings Castle stories.[2] Another is Percy Gorringe (pseudonym "Rex West"), whose willing intercession averted the danger that Bertie Wooster might be forced to marry Lady Florence Craye, herself an authoress.[3] Both of these two seem to have been writers of mysteries of the classic English style: but Jerry Vail, who intrudes inadvertently in the affairs of Lord Blandings and his pig, writes "hard-boiled" thrillers of the equally classic American mode. As a nonenthusiast for that form, I relish Wodehouse's comment that

> stories about New York private detectives, involving as they do almost no conscious cerebration, take very little time to write.[4]

Also to be found in Wodehouse's works are an array of criminals. Only a couple of them are really unpleasant; the crooked politician satisfactorily frustrated by the inimitable

---

[1] Wodehouse, *Uncle Dynamite*, p. 108.

[2] P.G. Wodehouse, *Something Fresh* (London: Methuen, 1915, 315 pp.) [U.S. title: *Something New*].

[3] P.G. Wodehouse, *Jeeves and the Feudal Spirit* (London: Herbert Jenkins, 1954, 222 pp.) [U.S. title: *Bertie Wooster Sees It Through*].

[4] P.G. Wodehouse, *Pigs Have Wings* (London: Herbert Jenkins, 1952, 220 pp.,), p. 59.

Psmith[1] and the blackmailing Heloise, Princess von und zu Dwornitzchek, unexpectedly casting her shadow across the otherwise cheerful plot of a much later novel.[2] Most others, though sufficiently morally reprehensible to deserve to be so amusingly frustrated, are fairly amiable creations. Of these, the prime examples are the smooth Gordon "Oily" Carlisle and his wife Gertrude "Sweetie"[3] and another husband-and-wife criminal team, Thos. G. "Soapy" and Dolly Molloy, together with the latter pair's sometime ally, sometime competitor Alexander "Chimp" Twist, alias J. Sheringham Adair.[4] Others are entirely endearing. The little New York burglar Spike Mullins set this style in Wodehouse's earliest "adult" novel, *A Gentleman of Leisure* (1910).[5] The next to appear was also a New Yorker—Bat Jarvis, the cat-loving leader of the Groome Street Gang, who became so helpfully entangled into Psmith's altruistic campaign in that city.[6] The purloining poetess Aileen Peavey and her inept inamorata, Edward Cootes, were to regret their entanglement with Psmith.[7] After that, the type became international and too numerous in Wodehouse's writings to itemize here, though two butler-burglars, the bibulous Phipps[8] and the beleaguered gangleader Horace Appleby,[9] perhaps merit special mention as exemplifying Wodehouse's gentle parodying of classic British mystery plots.

---

[1] P.G. Wodehouse, *Psmith Journalist* (London: A. & C. Black, 1915, 247 pp.). He is foreshadowed by Benjamin Scovell in *The Prince and Betty* (New York: Watt, 1912, 302 pp.); but Scovell's repentance makes him fractionally more endearing!

[2] P.G. Wodehouse, *Summer Moonshine* (London: Herbert Jenkins, 1938, 312 pp.).

[3] P.G. Wodehouse, *Hot Water* (London: Herbert Jenkins, 1932, 312 pp.), and *Cocktail Time* (London: Herbert Jenkins, 1958, 222 pp.).

[4] The Molloys and Twist appear first in P.G. Wodehouse, *Sam the Sudden* (London: Methuen, 1925, 248 pp.) [U.S. title: *Sam in the Suburbs*] and thereafter in five other novels.

[5] P.G. Wodehouse, *A Gentleman of Leisure* (London: Alston Rivers, 1912, 314 pp.) [U.S. title: *The Intrusions of Jimmy*].

[6] Wodehouse, *Psmith Journalist*.

[7] P.G. Wodehouse, *Leave it to Psmith* (London: Herbert Jenkins, 1928, 327 pp.).

[8] P.G. Wodehouse, *The Old Reliable* (London: Herbert Jenkins, 1951, 233 pp.).

[9] P.G. Wodehouse, *Do Butlers Burgle Banks?* (London: Herbert Jenkins, 1968, 189 pp.).

Though Bertie Wooster and many others play the amateur detective at times (usually, and entertainingly, with small success) professional detectives are not frequent in the Wodehouse canon. Indeed, only one springs to mind—Adrian Mulliner, a member of that numerous clan whose adventures were recounted at the Angler's Rest.[1] Of the many members of the official police forces of England, France, and the United States whom we encounter, none are in the least formidable—though the Paris Sergeant of Police in *Frozen Assets* (1964)[2] must cause a reminiscent *frisson* to pass down the spine of anyone who has encountered French bureaucracy at its tortuously obstructive worst! Moreover, most of these officers of the law suffer in varying degree from their attempts to contain the high spirits of Wodehouse's heroes and heroines. In a life where most of us have much to endure from the interferences of officialdom, it is delightful and cathartic to read of any twistings of their spiritual tails!

Yet the greatest benefit that Wodehouse derived—and thus, that we derive—from his reading of detective and mystery stories is its contribution to the colourful and elaborate weave of his plots. In his stories, as in classic crime fiction, whatever the vicissitudes the hero and heroine might undergo, we know that all will come right for them in the end—a particular comfort in a world where, in real life, there is no such guarantee. We who enjoy his writings may be wholeheartedly grateful for the breadth and quality of his reading in this literary genre.

---

[1] P.G. Wodehouse, "The Smile That Wins," in *Mulliner Nights* (London: Herbert Jenkins, 1933, 312 pp.), pp. 9–40.

[2] P.G. Wodehouse, *Frozen Assets* (London: Herbert Jenkins, 1964, 219 pp.) [U.S. title: *Biffen's Millions*].

Peter Rabe's Daniel Port

George Tuttle

As a reader of hardboiled thrillers, I've never been a big fan of series fiction. Series fiction has too many limits. Its plots revolve around the protagonist, his job, his friends, his beliefs, his habits, and his environment. There is a general lack of freedom and a certain amount of predictability in the stories. You know that the protagonist will win out in the end, just like you know how he and the other series regulars will react in certain situations. And because of the popularity of most series, authors tend to write and run them into the ground. They squeeze the series for every dollar that it's worth and keep adding on adventures long after the creative pool has dried up.

Yet despite this general dislike, I find Peter Rabe's Daniel Port stories rather enjoyable. Though they are not classics that will live on for eternity, they are worthwhile reads that lack many of the pitfalls of many series. First, whether it was his choice or not. Rabe didn't allow the series to run on and on. There are only five Port thrillers: *Dig My Grave Deep* (1956), *The Out is Death* (1957), *It's My Funeral* (1957), and *Time Enough to Die* (1959), all published by Fawcett Gold Medal. Port's adventures were never given the opportunity to become monotonous. Second, Port is by nature a free agent. He has no ties, no lasting friendships, no sidekicks, no job, and no permanent home. All Port has is his reputation as an ex-criminal, something that he can never shed, but he lacks many of the trappings and is atypical of the average series hero. Because of his free-agent quality, the Port thrillers don't read like typical series fiction. Third, Rabe is a talented storyteller, particularly when his protagonist has anti-hero characteristics. And Port, an ex-wonder boy of the Stoker Machine, is a morally ambiguous character in the best tradition of the hardboiled school.

The Port thrillers did not have a firecracker beginning. The first novel, *Dig My Grave Deep*, is the weakest effort in the series. The book, although well written, is too reminiscent of other stories where a protagonist kicks free of a corrupt political machine. The book will remind readers of a novel with a similar title by John (Cleve Adams) Spain. But *Dig My Grave Deep* does establish the character of Daniel Port, and from this less than fantastic beginning the series begins to take off. The next three in the series are much better. Anthony Boucher of the *New York Times*, in particular, gave all three high praise: *The Out is Death* is "noteworthy, . . . a barbed and bitter story, told with tension, objectivity, and powerful understatement"; *It's My Funeral* is "a peculiar and wryly entertaining sort of criminous comedy, mocking Hollywood, sex, cars, and crime itself among other cultural aspects of our age"; and *Bring Me Another Corpse* is "a taut and effectively understated story of intra and intergang politics."

But the fifth book in the series, *Time Enough to Die*, is the best and ends Port's endeavors on a strong not. The story opens in the small Mexican fishing village of Guanadera. Port has drifted into the village and initiated a relationship with a local girl named Maria. Port is enjoying himself and everything is going fine, until a friend of Maria, an old Japanese fisherman named Kiamoto, turns up missing and Maria asks Port's help in finding him.

The fact that there is a Japanese fisherman in Guanadera is not unusual. There are many Japanese in Guanadera; they migrated south from California. What is unusual (and what Port discovers) is that Kiamoto is not Japanese at all, but, rather, a Nationalist Chinese army general named Hoi Kio who has stolen one-and-a-half million dollars and is being hunted by a shady lawyer named d'Ortega and two agents of the American government named Briggs and Sanchez. All three suspect that Port knows more than he admits, because Port is a man with a reputation and former mob connections. Yet Port knows nothing. But he soon gets involved when Maria is beat up and then turns up missing, too.

Time Enough to Die has all the qualities of a solid thriller. The action is constant. The tension builds throughout the story. The setting is exotic (the village of Guanadera, the Mexican jungle, the ancient ruins and the waters off the coast give the story a colorful backdrop and provide it with a fitting place to end this series--fitting because it is logical that Port, a man trying to escape his reputation, would end up leaving the country). The characters are complex and intriguing.

The character of General Hoi Kio, the center of the conflict, is particularly compelling, a man vastly different from Port, yet strikingly similar. Hoi Kio comes from a totally different culture and background. As an army general for the Nationalist Chinese, he has little in common with Port. But like Port he is a man who wants out from the mindless world of pain, violence, and death, where good and evil often blend into one. Both Port and the general came to Guanadera to escape this world, and both, against their wills, have been drawn back into it. Although vastly different in character, Port and the general have been drawn together through a common experience. The general is an example of Rabe's ability to create realistic, three-dimensional characters. Rabe has a good sense of Oriental culture, as revealed in the general.

At the end, Rabe leaves Port with Maria in Mexico where he may eventually find peace. It seems proper that the ex-mob wonder boy from the East coast be left in a small village of Mexicans and Japanese, a place so different from his criminal roots.

Daniel Port is not Peter Rabe's best work. Rabe is the man who wrote *A House in Naples*, an anti-hero yarn that stands toe-to-toe with the best of Thompson, Williams, and Whittington. But Port is a good series that reflects Rabe's skill as a writer. As Mickey Spillane said of Rabe, "This guy is good!"

MYSTERY MOSTS: LONGEST TITLES

There have been some loooong Mystery titles!

Counting subtitles, a practice largely discontinued after the 1920s, titles consisting of twelve to fifteen words were fairly common. "Nat Ridley," like "EQ" and "Nick Carter" doubling both as author and hero, published fifteen books, all in 1926, almost all with subtitles, and thirteen of them with at least eight-word titles. The longest, *The Secret of the Stage: Or, Nat Ridley and the Bouquet of Death*, had thirteen. "Nat" can fairly be said to have published more books with rather long titles than anyone else. A pair of forerunners that surpassed him were Dick Donovan (1901) with *Jim the Penman* and Newton Newkirk (1904) with *Stealthy Steve, the Six-Eyed Sleuth*; with their subtitles (omitted here) both of these ran seventeen words. The real champs, though, were LeJemlys (1888), *The Millionaire's Folly: Or, The Beautiful Unknown: A Sensational Tale of Criminal Life from Facts Appearing on File in Records of Mooney & Bolend's Detective Agency* (twenty-six words), and Donovan again (!)_(1907), *The Shadow of Evil: In Which Is Narrated the Startling and Extraordinary History of James Mackoul, One of the Cleverest and Most Remarkable Rogues of His Age* (twenty-seven words). Besides the two Donovan titles given here, he had four others of at least ten words.

Of those without subtitles, Don Von Elsner (all of whose titles are clever—look 'em up in Hubin or Hagen) did three of eight words each. However, he was surpassed by several writers with single titles: *About the Murder of a Man Afraid of Women* (nine words) by Anthony Abbott; Jennie Melville and John Godey both produced ten-word titles; Charles Felton Pidgin did *Sarah Bernhardt Brown and What She Did in a Country Town* (eleven words); and the champ—Peter Van Greenway, with his twelve-worder, *The Man Who Held the Queen to Ransom and Sent Parliament Packing*. (Jeff Banks)

It's About Crime

Marvin Lachman

NOTES ON RECENT READING

It's feast or famine as far as short-story collections are concerned. Most of the year goes by with only a couple of monthly digest-sized magazines to provide my fix of the detective story in the format Poe intended. Then, as happened this fall, I'll get a batch of excellent anthologies within the space of a few weeks, and my faith in mankind is restored.

Death Locked In, published in trade paperback by International Polygonics, Ltd. (IPL) for $12.95 ($10.95 prior to 31 December 1987), is a generous collection of twenty-four stories covering 553 pages. Its editors, Robert C.S. Adey and Douglas G. Greene, are two of the world's leading experts on the locked room mystery. Lest those who are not devotees of the classical puzzle be put off, I will point out that this book contains great variety, though all stories have one common denominator: a locked room. From the pulps are stories by Fredric Brown and Cornell Woolrich. There is a science-fiction mystery by Anthony Boucher. Ngaio Marsh, quite appropriately, uses a theatrical setting. Even Bill Pronzini's nameless private eye solves one. Early locked-room stories by Thomas Bailey Aldrich, L. Frank Baum of Oz fame, Nick Carter, and Wilkie Collins are included. Finally, we have the best practitioners of this wonderful sub-genre: John Dickson Carr, Edward D. Hoch, and Ellery Queen with a reprint of one of his famous radio mysteries. Each story in the book has a learned introduction, telling interesting information about the author and putting the story into historical perspective.

Murder on the Aisle, the annual MWA anthology, has been edited by Mary Higgins Clark and published by Simon and Schuster in hardcover for $16.95. A surprisingly large number of mystery short stories have been set in theaters and sporting arenas, and Mrs. Clark has selected fifteen of the best, including "Moment of Decision," an outstanding story by Stanley Ellin, to whom this book is dedicated. Hoch has Captain Leopold solve a murder at the dog races, and Gerald Tomlinson sets a mystery at a football game. In one of my favorites, "A Break in the Film," by John F. Suter, we are in a small-town movie theater many years ago. The theater, as used for stage plays, is imaginatively used by Jon L. Breen and Thomas Adcock. Mr Adcock is one of the most talented new writers around, though I would appreciate a story in which he does not have his characters take cheap shots (not with guns) at President Reagan.

The MWA anthology, good as it is, should not be confused with the annual collection of the *best* stories of the previous year, *The Year's Best Mystery and Suspense Stories, 1987*, edited by Edward D. Hoch and published by Walker in hardcover for $17.95. Nineteen-Eighty-Six (this anthology is always a year behind) was a good year, and, while I would have included stories Mr. Hoch omitted, this is a very strong collection. For someone who does not normally read the short stories published in magazines each month, it is a *MUST*. Especially recommended is "Scalplock" by Clark Howard, who consistently manages to deal with current problems in his fiction without ever sacrificing storytelling or entertainment values. His story is probably the first mystery to deal with AIDS, and I doubt that a better one will ever be written on the subject.

There's certainly nothing current about William F. Nolan's *The Black Mask Boys*, whose most recent story was published in 1933. Yet, when I tell you that this is a collection of eight relatively unfamiliar stories from *Black Mask* by such giants as Carroll John Daly, Dashiell Hammett, Erle Stanley Gardner, Raoul Whitfield, Frederick Nebel, Horace McCoy, Paul Cain, and Raymond Chandler, you'll probably want to rush out and pick up Mysterious Press's $8.95 trade paperback reprint of it. Some stories are of special historical interest, e.g., an early Continental Op story from 1923 and Chandler's first pulp story, with an early version of Marlowe named Mallory. More important, all eight are, fifty-plus years after first publication, still eminently readable. Talk about passing the test of time. Nolan's bonuses include perceptive biographies of all the authors and complete check-lists of their *Black Mask* stories.

As I write this, ten days before Thanksgiving, the clowns of commerce are already peddling Christmas merchandise. Therefore, it suited my Scrooge-like heart to read Thomas Godfrey's excellent anthology of short stories, *Murder for Christmas*, published by Mysterious Press at $3.95. There are fourteen stories, and they are quite varied, with only the subject of the yuletide to connect them. Sherlock Holmes is included with "The Adventure of the Blue Carbuncle," and so is his logical successor, Ellery Queen, in "The Adventure of the Dauphin's Doll." We also have Poirot, Albert Campion, Maigret (in one of his best short cases), Father Brown, and Baroness Orczy's Lady Molly. Yet two non-series detective stories, by John Collier and Stanley Ellin, are probably the best in the whole book. Last, literally, with a funny cartoon on the last page, is the multi-talented Gahan Wilson, who gets us into the proper mood with a hilarious cover and other illustrations.

Single author collections of short stories are even rarer than anthologies, so we should be especially thankful for Joe L. Hensley's *Robak's Firm* (1987), a collection of fifteen tales from Doubleday priced at $12.95. More than half of the stories (eight, to be precise) have not appeared in print before. The others were in digest-sized magazines, but three were in that summer of 1984 reincarnation of the *Saint Mystery Magazine* which had so brief a life that if you blinked you missed it. Don't look for Hensley's series character, Donald Robak, to be in all the stories; in fact; he's not in most of them. Still, there is a series character named Cannert who is just as good. Several stories, not surprisingly, feature judges as characters. Hensley is, himself, a circuit court judge in Indiana. Based on the Hensley I've read, and *Robak's Firm* is a prime example, I'd even be willing to read Hensley's judicial opinions. They'd probably be fun.

There may be a lot of serial killers in real life, but do there have to be so many books about them in mystery fiction? *Fatal Reunion* (1987; Bantam, $3.95) involves the sequential murder of a group who were teen-age friends in the Bronx in the early 1960s. Having grown up in the Bronx, albeit earlier, I searched for signs of authenticity and found only a few, most of them regarding the borough's decay. Actually, most of the book takes place in Manhattan, Los Angeles, Atlantic City, and Oregon. If one is not travel-weary by the time one finishes it, one will be weary once again to have that old devil Vietnam as the motivation behind the killings. (No, I don't think I've spoiled any surprises should you, against my advice, read this book.)

As a Ngaio Marsh fan, I put aside her last mystery, *Light Thickens* (1982), unread, as a treat. Early in 1987 I did finally read it after I committed to doing the article about Dame Ngaio for DLB. I was pleased to find that, unlike Christie, Gardner, Queen, and many others, Marsh was as good at the end of her career as she had been almost fifty years before. The play, not the puzzle, is the thing in this book, which Jove has just reprinted ($2.95). The murder occurs quite late in the book, and the identity of the killer is relatively easy to discover. Motivation is not convincing. Ah, but in the writing about putting on a production of *MacBeth* I could almost smell the greasepaint. Marsh once said, without regret, that had se not spent as much time *directing* plays, especially Shakespeare, she could have *written* twice as many mysteries. If the time she spent in the theater is responsible for books as good as *Light Thickens*, then she made the right choice.

Robert B. Parker's Spenser concedes he is a smart ass, admitting, regarding his penchant for wise cracks, that "it's a bad habit, I know, but sometimes I can't resist." I can't resist the Spenser series and thoroughly enjoyed *Early Autumn* (1981), reprinted by Dell ($3.95), although it also has few mystery elements. As in the previous book in the series, *Looking for Rachel Wallace* (1980), the firstnameless detective functions more as a bodyguard than a sleuth. He's also a surrogate father and guidance counsellor in a book which is mostly about his efforts to help a teenager grow up. While I am not a big fan of the species teenager, I did root for Paul Giacomin, because his parents were a pretty slimy couple. This lightning-paced book was fun to read, and, after all, do we always need mystery in our mysteries?

Carroll and Graf's recent reprinting of Dorothy B. Hughes's *The Expendable Man* (1963) makes us realize it has been about a quarter of a century since she last published a novel. (She did publish a biography of Erle Stanley Gardner in 1978.) As those who saw her at Bouchercon 1987 are aware, she still appears hale and hearty, so there is reason to hope for more fiction. *The Expendable Man* is not only a fine crime novel, it is also a book which dissects with acute verbal precision America's customs and mores of the early 1960s. No one in the mystery field has written better regarding Arizona; only Fredric Brown wrote as well. Regarding mystery plots, I believe in saying as little as possible. Having read blurbs and reviews which spoiled the surprises of *The Expendable Man*, I am convinced I am right. Enough said.

There has been considerable speculation about the roles John Rhode and Carter Dickson (John Dickson Carr) played in their collaboration, *Fatal Descent* (1939), reprinted in a typically attractive and sturdy trade paperback by Dover for $4.95. Because his name comes first, I suspect the basic plot was Rhodes', with Carr providing the mechanics of an ingenious impossible crime. Here we have murder committed in the equivalent of a doubly locked room, since a publishing tycoon is found murdered in a sealed elevator in a sealed elevator shaft. Because Rhodes was not known for his humor, I also suspect Carr is responsible for the book's many light moments, especially the wonderful byplay between Chief Inspector Hornbeam and Police Surgeon Horace Glass. The latter is always looking for psychological explanations, and when the somewhat naive Inspector thinks a word Glass has used—nymphomania—has to do with stealing things in a department store, we get a truly hilarious line. I'd be surprised if Rhode, even if his life depended upon it, could have come up with that one. But enough of this meting out credit. This is a joint effort which works so well it tells us why the Golden Age of the detective puzzle glistened so brightly.

As I write these words, Public Television (bless it!) is doing three Dorothy L. Sayers mysteries on *Mystery!* Not surprisingly, the books—*Strong Poison* (1930), *Have His Carcase* (1932), and *Gaudy Night* (1936), have been made available in paperback. The publisher is Harper's Perennial Mystery Library, and each volume is $4.50. The common thread running through the books is Lord Peter Wimsey's wooing of mystery writer Harriet Vane, clearly a stand-in for Sayers herself. The romantic elements do not detract at all from the mystery. If anything, they might make Wimsey more bearable for those (not I) who find him insufferable. The first two books are relatively conventional, albeit strong mysteries. *Gaudy Night* is something else again, a book which was hotly debated during the 1930s because it contains no murder. Some claimed there was not even a crime. I say this is Sayers' best book and as good a book with an academic setting as I've ever read. The paperback edition is 457 pages long, and I found every one of them replete with suspense and intelligence.

It has been too long (more than a dozen years) since there

was a paperback reprint of Michael Innes's *One-Man Show* (1952) available in this country, and I hope some publisher will heed these words and remedy the situation. This is a book I can recommend even though Innes is a bit less disciplined than usual and his sleuth, John Appleby, is a trifle more snobbish. It starts with the murder of a painter but midway evolves into one of Innes's longer chase sequences. Still, it is a book with many surprises. There are jokes, as when after a modern painting is stolen, Appleby suggests the newspapers write about it as the mystery of the abstracted abstraction. When the murder victim's blood drips onto a statue, someone thinking of police forensic work says, "Blood is the one thing you can't get out of a stone." Yet, Appleby shows considerable compassion for the victim and for a missing woman whose privacy he feels he has violated when he must search her room, quoting Thomas Hardy: "And all her shining keys will be took from her, and her cupboards opened; and little things a' didn't wish seen, anybody will see." Appleby is absent from the "stage" for long stretches of the book, but his place is admirably taken by his wife, doing some detective work of her own, and a character new to the series, his prissy assistant, Detective-Inspector Cadover.

Seldom has a mystery had a sicker bunch of people than Jonathan Kellerman's *Blood Test* (1986), reprinted by Signet at $4.50. Child psychologist Alex Delaware has been called in to help a small boy who has lymphoma and must remain in isolation while undergoing chemotherapy because it will temporarily damage his immune system and make him susceptible to infections. The child is kidnapped, and his strange-acting parents and a group of religious cultists (the book is set in Southern California, where else?) are suspected. Alex is especially concerned because the treatment is the only chance to save the child's life. At the same time, he is being harassed by an irate father against who he testified during a messy divorce hearing. The father was unfit to see his children until he underwent psychotherapy. Delaware is more the psychologist in this book than in his Edgar-winning debut, *When the Bough Breaks*, in which he functioned more like the standard private eye. He uses his profession, especially the history he takes before exam and treatment, to detect. Kellerman keeps piling up the psychopaths, also giving us explicit sexual descriptions which seldom give the reader credit for imagination, and frequent use of drugs. Yet, he is a compelling story-teller, and it is hard not to want to know what will happen to a very appealing five-year-old who is not only a victim of cancer but is being used by a group of obnoxious adults.

Almost half a century passed between Margery Allingham's *The Fashion in Shrouds* (1938) and Marian Babson's *Death in Fashion* (1986). Both have been reprinted by Bantam, the Babson book scheduled for December 1987 publication at $2.95. The difference between the two books tells us something about how readers' tastes have evolved. Now, there is little call for the kind of leisurely, sophisticated dialogue that made Allingham such a pleasure to read. Yet, on its own terms, *Death in Fashion* is quite a good book, fast-paced and capturing the excitement and tawdriness of London in the 1980s as murder takes place in one of its leading fashion houses during the week in which buyers are being shown the new line. The clothing industry has not been background in many mysteries, and Babson, a transplanted American who lives in England, handles her subject well and provides a very readable book.

Will success spoil Brock "the Rock" Callahan? Apparently, to judge by William Campbell Gault's *The Dead Seed* (1985), reprinted by Charter at $2.95. He's retired on money left him by a wealthy uncle, but since he's bored he helps his police detective friend, Bernie Vogel, investigate a crime involving the Callahans' next-door neighbors. Gault seems to have injected Callahan with tired blood, and some of the dialogue over cocktails between Brock and his wife, Jan, sounds like road company Nick and Nora. The plot is slow and too reminiscent of Ross Macdonald, with a seventeen-year-old boy troubled by events which happened long in the past. That California standby, the religious cult, turns up, but it is about as exotic as mashed potatoes. All is not lost for Gault fans, however. Callahan is still one of the best of the first-person narrators, and the Callahan-Vogel relationship alone is worth the price of the book, with some funny bits regarding literary quotations.

DEATH OF A MYSTERY WRITER

STUART BUCHAN, in Pittsfield, Massachusetts, on 15 October 1987, at age forty-five. Born in Australia, Buchan was reared in Singapore, Scotland, and Vancouver. Though he wrote many short stories and two mainstream novels, his only mystery was *Fleeced* (1975).

IRVE TUNICK, in Carmel, New York, on 5 September 1987, at age seventy-five. He was former president of the Eastern Region of the Television Writers of America and wrote scripts for many television series, including *Ironside, Witness,* and *The F.B.I.* He also wrote a feature film, *Murder, Inc.* (1960).

(GEORGE) EMLYN WILLIAMS, in London on 25 September 1987 at age eighty-one. While he was best known as the author and star of the award-winning 1938 play *The Corn Is Green*, which was set in his native Wales, he was also active in crime writing. His first play, *A Murder Has Been Arranged*, was produced in 1930. His 1935 play *Night Must Fall*, about a psychopath who may be carrying a severed head in a hat box, was an enormous hit in London and then New York, with Williams in the leading role. (Robert Montgomery played the part in the U.S. film version.) Williams also wrote *Beyond Belief*, a true crime book about Ian Brady and Myra Hindley, the notorious British child-murderers.

Reel Murders

Walter Albert

Books on film continue to pour from the commercial and university presses, but very few of them have made their way to my reference shelf. The text I use most often is Leonard Maltin's annual TV Movies and Video Guide, and the 1988 edition showed up in local bookstores in October. This edition is a thick, 1150-page, paperbound volume and one of the things I like about it is that, while new titles are constantly being added, Maltin prides himself on not deleting older films. This means that many films are listed that are not currently available, but, as Maltin points out in his introduction, other films (like "Animal Crackers" or "Animal Kingdom") that were once out of circulation are available again and, besides, confesses Maltin, "I just can't bear to drop a film once we've listed it in the book." The major change over the past few years, aside from the abominable alphabetization system which Maltin at least has the courage to admit "differs" from that of other books, has been that the book has become—according to the jacket copy—the "essential reference for home video rental." This does not mean that sources are listed for films available on video, but this is an acknowledgement of the tremendous revolution in home video viewing.

As far as I can tell, Maltin does not includes films that have never been available to TV stations, and this means that titles transferred from 16 mm. film to videocassette are not recorded. One of the most exciting developments in video cassettes in the last few years has been the transfer of obscure titles to to videocassette. Sinister Cinema, of Pacifica, California, has been very active and, tempted by their ad, I recently ordered "Drums of Jeopardy," a 1931 Tiffany Pictures release starring Warner Oland as "Boris Karlov," an increasingly unbalanced doctor seeking revenge for his daughter's death. This film is described at some length in the Turner/Price Forgotten Horrors (A. S. Barnes, 1979), but this invaluable guide to the Poverty Row productions of the 1930s is silent on what Sinister Cinema advertised as a pre-"Cat and the Canary" thriller, "Midnight Faces," circa 1926. What they did not advertise is that this is a spoof of old-dark-house thrillers before the genre was established, and there are enough hidden passages, clawed hands appearing out of solid walls, and red herrings to satisfy any fan of this once-popular entertainment. Oh, to fly off on the wings of a bat to the country for a murderous weekend of chills and thrills! But the most recent exhuming of "The Cat and the Canary," by director Radley Metzger, was a sanitized, cobweb-free reconsideration, well-lighted and with none of the proper trappings.

If you're looking for some respite from pictures that move, my recommendation for the art/movie book of the year is John Canemaker's sumptuous Winsor McCay (Abbeville, 1987), which includes a chapter on the innovative animation techniques of this important film pioneer. However, a special award of merit should be given to Lobby Cards: The Classic Films (Los Angeles: Pomegranate Press). The reproductions in this attractive volume range in date from 1919 ("Broken Blossoms") to 1943 ("Casablanca"). The seventy-nine cards are from the collection of Michael Hawks, and, while some of them are of interest chiefly for their rarity or for the stars, many of them are attractively designed and there is, in particular, a generous sampling from the great horror films of the 20s and 30s. Colors are often garish and not notable for their subtlety, but among my favorites here are cards for "Phantom of the Opera," "The Unholy Three," "Dracula," "King Kong," "The Wizard of Oz," "The Prince and the Pauper," and "Alice in Wonderland" (1933). I would be hard put to it to choose a favorite, although the bold lettering of "The Virginia" is striking and the card for "The Mummy" is impressive. If you already have Foyer Pleasure, a collection of lobby cards published in 1982, you needn't worry about duplication. I couldn't find a single instance of a duplicate card, and the layout of the 1987 volume is superior to that of the earlier book. The border design was omitted in FP, but in LC the cards are inset with a white space framing the card. Not inexpensive at $29.95, but a feast for the movie buff's eye.

William Everson's More Classics of the Horror Film (Citadel, 1986) is a fine belated gift for the movie buff--in spite of the lamentable absence of an index--but Phil Hardy's The Encyclopedia of Horror Movies (Harper and Row, 1986), with its sensible organization by year, and with a complete end-of-volume index, is my recommendation over the Everson, if a choice has to be made. "Midnight Faces" is not included, but, after years of anxious searching for information, I find in it an entry on "The Smiling Ghost" (1941), which I remember with particular pleasure from my childhood as a scary mystery/horror film. Hardy says that "script, direction and camera work are all surprisingly good," but when you look at the cast list you will quickly recognize this as a fairly classy entry. It features Wayne Morris, Brenda Marshall, Lee Patrick, Alexis Smith, and Alan Hale, and I suspect that this is one Warner Brothers film that deserves a quick reissue by a video company or prime-time showings on TVs "American Movie Classics."

Brenda Marshall reminds me that one of the most enjoyable sessions at the 1987 Bouchercon was a showing (to an audience of about five people) of Lloyd Bacon's fast-paced, amusing

"Footsteps in the Dark" (1941). This starred Errol Flynn as a mystery writer who gets involved in a real-life murder mystery, much to the dismay of his wife (Brenda Marshall) and his grande dame mother (Lucille Watson). This also features Lee Patrick and Alan Hale and I can't remember seeing a more entertaining comedy-mystery recently. Movies really were better in the "old" days.

MYSTERY MOSTS: COMICBOOK HEROES

Comicbooks! They used to be everywhere—as much a part of the "throwaway" print culture as the pulps—and while they haven't quite disappeared, they are now scarce and expensive and people are collecting them every bit as seriously as one might collect Christie first editions, paperbacks with McGinnis covers, or all books featuring Nero Wolfe.

Since they started, comicbooks have included some heroes of interest to the mystery fan. So, naturally, the question arises: What detective hero has had the most comics published under his name? (The other questions—which has appeared in the most stories, which has occupied the most pages, and which had the greatest popularity—are unanswerable?)

The easy—and arguably correct—answer would be Superman. There have been well over four hundred *Superman* comics published, and they are still going strong—or what passes for that these days. But while he is/has been primarily a "crime fighter," he is also undeniably a superhero. So let's don't count him. Batman is also a rather obvious choice, closing in on four hundred books. While he has no disturbing "super powers" or off-world origin, he is still a costume hero. So we will rule him out, too.

Next most prominent is our old friend Dick Tracy, who began with a McKay Featurebook in January 1938 and had most of his appearances in the 125-issue Dell (and, latterly, Harvey) monthly. counting "giveaways" and "Black & Whites," Tracy appeared in 154 comics named for himself in all, clearly leading all challengers.

If you're such a purist that a hero with comicstrip origins is unacceptable even in a discussion of comicbooks, then Doc Savage is the champ (twenty Street & Smith comics plus others from Gold Key and Marvel for a total of thirty-nine). Of course, his "big brother" at S&S, The Shadow, racked up 127 (also from three different publishers), but he was a costume hero.

Still not pure enough for you? Well, Charlie Chan had a total of twenty-three from four different publishers; and if you would disqualify him because they were based on the B-movie series rather than Biggers' original creation, we are going to be dealing in really smallish numbers. In fact, the leader of the rest and the only other book detective hero whose total number of comic books runs to two digits is The Saint. He appeared in twelve. (Jeff Banks)

Verdicts

Book Reviews

L.R. Wright. *The Suspect*. Penguin, 1987, 217 pp., $3.95.

The cover of the Penguin edition of *The Suspect* promises everything. Not only has the mandatory comparison with Ruth Rendell and P.D. James been blazoned above L.R. Wright's name, but also a banner heading just below the title informs us that the novel won an Edgar. Happily, Wright is a very good writer who meets all the expectations Penguin's public relations people raise.

An inverted mystery, *The Suspect* introduces Karl Alberg, Staff Sergeant of the Royal Canadian Mounted Police, and Cassandra Mitchell, a local librarian, apparently the featured characters in a proposed series--that is, if the publication of two novels suggests a series, and I hope it does. Conventionally, both Alberg and Mitchell, single and restless, have come to turning points in their lives; less conventionally, perhaps, they attempt to dispel loneliness by consulting the personal columns of the local newspaper. It's a tribute to Wright's skill that within minutes after she has introduced us to these competent, pleasant, decent people, we know them well enough to realize the depths of their loneliness because we understand how very uncharacteristic their ventures into the lonely hearts columns are.

Both Karl Alberg and Cassandra Mitchell sometimes serve as the novel's central consciousness, as does the third major character, George Wilcox, suspected of murdering his neighbor and former brother-in-law, Carlyle Burke. Alberg likes the elderly Wilcox but believes he must be punished if he is, in fact, the killer. Cassandra Mitchell cherishes a sweet friendship with George and is attracted to Karl; she cannot balance her wish that George be spared further suffering (he is recently widowed) against Karl's obvious duty. George reluctantly recognizes Karl's honesty but fears his professional skill and is angered by Alberg's unwavering pursuit. Because all three of these strong characters are thoughtful people, the conflicts between their desires and their duties are numerous, painful, and wholly persuasive.

Equally convincing is Wright's portrait of Canada's "Sunshine Coast" (the Sechelt Peninsula), and of the town of Sechelt, where "there are traffic accidents to deal with, and occasional vandalism, and petty theft, and some drunkenness now and then. There is very seldom a murder." Presumably, if a series is in the making, the incidence of murder in Sechelt will

Verdicts (Book Reviews)

rise, at least in Wright's fictive rendering of that city. Her understated blend of the factual (geography, weather patterns) and the fictional (her characters and her plots) is one of Wright's great strengths and is but one evidence of her generally pleasing style. The infrequent flaws in that style do very, very little to diminish the impact of *The Suspect*; in fact, when Wright does err, it's usually because she doesn't trust herself enough: "She touched an iris, and the light stroke of her finger against the petal of the flower suggested to Alberg his own gesture to brush closed Carlyle Burke's eyelid; there was a great gentleness in it." No need to mention the gentleness; we feel it in the tone and texture of the prose. As a matter of fact, we feel her characters' concurrent gentleness and toughness and vulnerability in almost every scene, in almost every gesture L.R. Wright describes. I hope she's planning a very long series. (Jane S. Bakerman)

Agatha Christie. *Curtain* and *Sleeping Murders*. Two posthumous publications by Agatha Christie, now in their umpteenth printings and available in book stores and supermarkets everywhere.

Hercule Poirot, the conceited Belgian super-sleuth with the egg-shaped head and waxed moustache, whose "little grey cells" were the nemesis of clever criminals for over half a century, is dead.

Created by Agatha Christie in her first detective novel, *The Mysterious Affair at Styles* (1920), both the author and her intuitive investigator evolved gradually into a phenomenon.

Miss Christie has written a number of acknowledged masterpieces in the suspense genre, including: *The Murder of Roger Ackroyd* (1926), *Murder in the Calais Coach* (1934), *The ABC Murders* (1935), *Death on the Nile* (19376), *And Then There Were None* (1939), and *Death Comes as the End* (1944).

Her books are best-sellers in numerous languages and are read by more people than any other literary works, with the exception of the Bible and Shakespeare's plays. She had successes on the stage (with *Ten Little Indians*, *Witness for the Prosecution* [the only mystery play to win both the New York Critics Circle Award and the Antoinette Perry Award as the best foreign play of the year], and *The Mousetrap* [still running in London after more than thirty-five years]), in the movies (*Murder on the Orient Express*, *Death on the Nile*), and on television (*Murder Is Easy*, *The Moving Finger*).

There are very few instances in suspense fiction in which the series detective, who appears in a succession of books, thus building a following among the reading public, is killed by the author. Arthur Conan Doyle, becoming bored with Sherlock Holmes, sent him and his arch-enemy Moriarty to a swift end at the Reichenbach Falls, only to have to yield to public pressure and revive him in another series of short stories. Henry Poggioli, Ph.D., a psychologist teaching at Ohio State University, acted as an amateur detective in a series of short stories collected into the volume *Clues of the Caribbees* (1929) by T.S. Stribling and ended in a bizarre, unexpected death. Drury Lane, ex-actor, aging and deaf investigator created by Ellery Queen (under the pseudonym Barnaby Ross) in some excellent novels (*The Tragedy of X*, 1932; *The Tragedy of Y*, 1932; and *The Tragedy of Z*, 1933), has gone to his maker in the appropriately named fourth book of the series, *Drury Lane's Last Case* (1933). Dutch Commissioner Van der Valk's shining career came to an abrupt end in *Aupre de ma Blonde* (1972) after a number of successful novels by Nicholas Freeling. And now, curtains for another hero-detective who caught the fancy of the public.

Hercule Poirot, pensioned from the Belgian police force and a refugee during World War I, was hoping to retire and concentrate on growing vegetables in the English countryside, but a life of leisure was not in the cards, as he was drawn to solve a number of difficult cases.

A disciple of Poe's C. Auguste Dupin, Poirot's theory of deduction is: Crime must be solved by "the little grey cells" rather than by physical evidence like fingerprints, footprints, or cigarette ashes. Thus he is less a man of action than an observer of human nature. This is evident in *Curtain* more than in previous cases. Here Poirot is literally an armchair detective, hearing the news from his perennial side-kick, Captain Hastings, putting two and two together while hardly leaving his room. His unknown antagonist is an ingenious and sadistic murderer-by-suggestion who subtly convinces other people, vulnerable by nature, to carry out the actual bloody deeds under his diabolical influence.

The book is leisurely paced, concentrating in a lengthy exposition of the characters assembled at Styles Court, pinpointing the brewing undercurrents, culminating in two violent deaths. As is usual with Christie, there are a few suspects congregated under one roof, the scattering of various clues whose significance is not initially clear (the play "Othello," a pair of binoculars, a bottle of sleeping tablets, a set of duplicate keys, a wig and false moustache, a bullet hole in the center of the victim's forehead), some acute psychological observations, a double-twist solution, and a wallop of an ending.

Hercule Poirot—a comic figure with his small physical stature, broken English, and passion for symmetry. Hercule Poirot—unmarried, neatly dressed, vegetarian. Hercule Poirot—one of the most conceited detectives in the genre ("My name is Hercule Poirot. I am probably the greatest detective in the world"). Hercule Poirot—man of sentiment, flourish, and bravado. In spite of his eccentricities, or perhaps because of them, he will be remembered as the gallant knight of law and order, one of the greatest detectives of all time.

Miss Jane Marple—tall, thin, with blue eyes and white hair—was born in the village of St. Mary Mead. The universally beloved spinster lives in a small house on a meager fixed income, is prone to gossip, and pursues the hobbies of gardening and knitting. She is attempting to keep up with the times but deplores the disappearance of a more genteel era. Her observations of life in a country village have given her an uncanny gift

Verdicts (Book Reviews)

for fathoming human nature. Her ability to draw analogies between current dilemmas and past events in St. Mary Mead is an important tool in her indefatigable sleuthing career.

Miss Marple's maiden appearance was in *Murder at the Vicarage* (1930). Among her more celebrated cases were *The Tuesday Club Murders* (1932), *The Body in the Library* (1942), *A Murder Is Announced* (1950), *What Mrs. McGillicuddy Saw!* (1957), *At Bertram's Hotel* (1965), and *Nemesis* (1971).

Altogether, she graced the pages of sixteen novels and short-story collections and was the heroine of four well received British films starring the late Margaret Rutherford.

And now, *Sleeping Murder.* While the work is not as original or innovative as some of Christie's masterpieces, it is nonetheless an excellent example of plotting and misdirection.

A charming young couple from New Zealand, who had just bought a Victorian villa at a seaside resort, are determined to solve a macabre strangulation that took place eighteen years before. Under the guidance of Miss Marple they uncover long forgotten family skeletons, evil passions are reawakened, and a dormant murderer strikes again.

The author's craftsmanship is admirable. Every chapter serves as a piece that fits comfortably into a gigantic jigsaw puzzle. There is no padding. There is an easy flow of action towards an inevitable climax. The author deftly scatters the "red herrings" and the legitimate clues but plays a fair game with the reader. The solution is not as surprising nor as overwhelming as that of *Curtain*, Hercules Poirot's last case, but it still adheres to the author's trademark of making her criminal the least-likely person.

Agatha Christie, who passed away a few years ago at the age of eighty-five, left behind a phenomenal success and eighty-seven treasured books. Both *Curtain* and *Sleeping Murder* are worthy epitaphs. And yet, somehow, one has a hunch, a vision, of more posthumous works by one of the most popular authors of the twentieth century who may have passed away—but who simply refuses to die. (Amnon Katatchnik)

Ed McBain. *Poison.* Arbor House, 263 pp., $16.95.

Is Marilyn Hollis killing her lovers? One by one the bodies are piling up as various attractive men are being murdered. The only thing the victims have in common is that at one time they all knew Marilyn Hollis intimately.

The detectives at the 87th Precinct are on the trail of a vicious murderer in *Poison*, the latest entry in the longest, and arguably the best, police procedural series.

The ratiocinative tale of detection was created by Edgar Allan Poe in the early 1940s, embellished by Arthur Conan Doyle at the turn of the century, and flowered into the Golden Age of detective fiction a few decades later.

In the 1920s and 1930s, Dashiell Hammett and a group of other writers associated with *Black Mask Magazine* began the realistic, hard-boiled school of detective fiction, in which a weathered private eye took over the place of the brilliant amateur.

Then, in the late 1940s and early 1950s, another kind of story began to appear—the police procedural—in which the mystery is solved by regular police detectives utilizing authentic, real-life methods.

The series's starkly realistic tales, blanketed by a wacky comic spirit, are concerned with various crimes mingled with social problems. Muggers, kidnappers, rapists, snipers, and drug pushers are among the criminals roaming the streets of the mythical island of Isola.

The disclaimer page of every 87th Precinct novel assures the readers that "the city in these pages is imaginary. The people, the places are all fictitious." But there is no doubt that the "imaginary city" is characteristic of Manhattan.

As is customary with the police procedural subgenre, there is no single hero in the series. The protagonist is a team, the whole squad. They go through daily police routines, check evidence methodically, interrogate witnesses, use informants, tail suspects, utilize the resources of the laboratory. It is the author's versatile topics, ironic twists, and narrative skills—notably poetic images and slapstick humor—that lift the mundane proceedings to exciting, suspenseful heights.

Among the prominent members of the squad are detective Steve Carella, whose beautiful wife, Teddy, is a deaf-mute; detective Meyer Meyer, whose father thought it would be amusing to give his son the same first name and surname; detective Cotton Hawes, a giant of a man with a white streak in his hair; detective Andy Parker, a braggart and a sadist; detective Bert Kling, the naive rookie of the early stories; and Lieutenant Peter Byrnes, the fatherly commander of the Precinct.

And then there is Hal Wallis, the diminutive, wiry detective who, in *Poison*, has broken the cardinal rule of police work: never fall in love with a suspect.

Marilyn Hollis draws him like a dangerous siren, protesting her innocence, slowly confessing her sordid past. This is a case in which the investigative cop himself becomes entangled in a web of violent passions.

McBain's talent for hooking the reader's attention is evident from the very first page: "The two Homicide detectives peered cautiously at the dead body on the carpet.... Monoghan and Monroe were both wearing dark suits with vests. They were wearing dark overcoats and dark fedoras. Their faces were ruddy from the bitter March cold outside. They were both holding handkerchiefs to their noses because of the stench of vomit and fecal matter in the apartment...."

The author's gift for concocting plausible events, offbeat characters, gritty detail, and gallows humor has earned him the titles "the Norman Rockwell of the police procedural" and "King of the police procedural." That's high praise indeed in a field that boasts such luminary writers as John Creasey, Hillary Waugh, Nicholas Freeling, Bill Knox, James McClure, Colin Wilcox, and Elizabeth Linington. (Amnon Kabatchnik)

Hedman-Morelius, Iwan. *Kriminalliterature pa Svenska 1749-1985*
[Crime fiction in Sweden 1749-1985]. Dast Forlag, 1986.
473pp. ISBN 91-85208-078.

This the third, revised edition of a bibliography originally published in 1971 and 1974. The 40,000 books--a considerable increase over the 15,000 titles in the second edition--are listed by author and title. The title index of the second edition has been incorporated into the body of the work and bunches of titles are listed among the author headings, a somewhat confusing policy for someone using the work for the first time. It would have been helpful to have the alphabetical listing of titles set off in some way in the text or, even more desirable, given as a separate index, but this editorial decision does not seriously impede consultation of the volume.

Swedish translations of foreign language titles are paired with the original edition, and some English language titles are included for which there do not appear to be Swedish translations. The number of titles included is a testament to the interest in detective fiction in Sweden and, even though the introduction and other editorial comments are in Swedish, the bibliography offers reasonably easy access to the reader unfamiliar with Swedish and is a substantial contribution to the reference library. Information on purchasing the book may be obtained by writing to the editor at Hulan, Lyckas Gard, S561 90 Husquarna, Sweden. (Walter Albert)

Philip MacDonald. *Mystery at Friar's Pardon.* Doubleday, 1932; Collins, 1931, as by Martin Porlock.

Friar's Pardon, built in the reign of King James the Second, had had five mysterious deaths of the owners of the house. In the last one, a doctor swore that the owner had died of drowning, though he was upstairs and there was no water in or near the room and no evidence of water on his clothes or person.

Despite these overtones of the supernatural, Mrs. Enid Lester-Greene, best-selling author of, among other titles, *Sir Galahad Comes Home*, *Oasis Love*, and *Paradise for Two*, buys the house and plans to occupy the room where the mysterious deaths took place as her study. She does this in the face of warnings by friends and family and despite reports of a sometimes mischievous and sometimes nasty poltergeist active in the house.

All this build-up would be rather disappointing if nothing happened to Mrs. Lester-Greene, so something does. In a locked room, about four minutes after having made a phone call crying for help, Mrs. Lester-Greene is found dead, drowned, according to the medical examiner, though there is no water in the room.

The solution to the locked-room aspect will probably be familiar to those who read widely in that subgenre, and the murderer may be a little too evident to the reader, but not to the police, who lean toward the supernatural explanation.

An interesting amateur detective—the recently hired estate steward who never has a chance to do any of the work for which he is employed—the unusual murder method, a fair amount of the occult, and some amusing minor characters make this a novel well worth finding. And since the supernatural, or what seems the supernatural, plays a significant role in the crime, the seance to ask the murdered woman who and how is a fitting climax. (William F. Deeck)

Philip MacDonald. *Persons Unknown*. Doubleday, 1931; Collins, 1932, as *The Maze*; White Circle Books, no date, as *The Maze*, 251 pages.

In his introduction to this documentary novel, Philip MacDonald says: "In this book I have striven to be absolutely fair to the reader. There is *nothing*—nothing at all—for the detective that the reader has not had. More, the reader has had his information in exactly the same form as the detective—that is, the verbatim report of evidence and question."

Anthony Gethryn is vacationing in Costa del Chica, Spain, when he receives from Assistant Commissioner Sir Egbert Lucas, C.I.D., the transcript of the coroner's inquest into the death of Maxwell Brunton. Brunton had been murdered in his study one night, a crime that could have been committed only by someone residing in the house. Brunton, according to the testimony, was a philanderer and a man easily given to anger, but he also had many good points.

Of the residents, some, particularly Brunton's wife and son, had strong motives for doing him in. Others had weak or no discernible motives. The police investigation and the testimony at the inquest lead to no conclusion as to who might have committed the murder and why.

It was Sir Egbert's hope, although not his expectation, that Gethryn would be able to spot the murderer. Gethryn's usual rule is to look for "oddnesses" in a case when he can find them; in this one, he finds many oddnesses. So Gethryn turns the process upside down and spots the culprit, who, he points out, will never be convicted by an English court.

I didn't spot the killer, but I should have, although the motive, unusual for a book of this vintage, would still have eluded me. Mystery novels don't come any fairer-play than this one. (William F. Deeck)

Anthony Abbot. *The Shudders*. Farrar & Rinehart, 1944, 306 pages.

"The author requests that in discussing *The Shudders* readers and reviewers do not give away its plot." An understandable request by Anthony Abbot (who in reality was Fulton Oursler), one must admit, since the plot is asinine. Still, a reviewer must mention something about the book, besides declaiming that Anthony Abbot, the narrator and Watson for

Verdicts (Book Reviews)

Thatcher Colt, is an even bigger twit than S.S. Van Dine, the narrator and Watson for Philo Vance, which is a claim many won't believe until they encounter Abbot the narrator.

Briefly then—and I hope that Abbot's shade does not come back to haunt me—Thatcher Colt, New York City Police Commissioner, more detective than administrator, has been responsible for the conviction of a villain who poisoned his boss and mentor and made off with two million never-located dollars. The evening he is to be executed, the poisoner asks Colt to visit with him. He warns Colt that an even greater villain—a Dr. Baldwin—who kills for sport and who kills undetectably is lurking about ready to do untold damage.

The poisoner is executed, with Colt looking on, and then Colt begins an unsuccessful three-year search for Baldwin. One day the former warden of the prison at which the poisoner was executed rushes into Colt's office to tell him that he has met Dr. Baldwin, that the poisoner's executioners are dying off, and that the warden is to be next. He also has more important information to impart, but he's too busy talking about side issues to do so, and then he dies—of apparently natural causes.

Why is Dr. Baldwin seemingly avenging the executed poisoner? It's all too silly and impossible to narrate, even if the author's request was to be flouted even more than I have already. Skip this one. (William F. Deeck)

Hugh Austin. *The Milkmaid's Millions.* Charles Scribner's Sons, 1948, 181 pages.

This is the second and apparently last in the "Sultan's Harem" mysteries. The Sultan is Wm (that's the way he spells it) Sultan, the only surviving member of Sultan, Sultan & Sultan, counselors at law. Wm is thirty-five years old, but talks and thinks as if he were in his seventies. His staff, all female and thus "the harem," treats him as if he were their grandfather, though his secretary appears to regard him as a possible swain.

Wm's main interest in life is compiling his late uncle's "Life & Letters." His staff is typing up the forty-second chapter of the second volume, which seems to comprise the twenty-seven thank-you letters the uncle sent for presents received on his fourteenth birthday. One shudders to think what the other forty-one chapters in volume two might consist of, and volume one doesn't bear thinking about at all.

One of Wm's few clients has prepared a codicil to his will, having recently discovered a direct descendant, and Wm is called upon to prove the *bona fides* of the new family member. Shortly after Wm arrives at the client's home, however, the testator is murdered. The investigators think that Wm did it, evidence arises that Wm probably didn't do it, and then new developments seem to demonstrate that he did indeed do it.

Wm's harem, who were responsible for his getting involved in the mess, arrives on the scene to vamp some of the suspects and rig some evidence so that Wm will not be convicted of the crime.

Those who enjoy the pedantic and stuffy, mixed with the preposterous, will find this novel delightful. The crime's rather good, too. (William F. Deeck)

Blanche Bloch. *The Bach Festival Murders*. Harper and Brothers, 1942, 289 pages.

Can Crescent City handle a Bach festival, particularly when it conflicts with the season of its not very popular symphony orchestra? One would think not, especially when the symphony orchestra's old conductor has been removed and a new conductor, a man very jealous of his wife, has been installed at the request of his wife's old flame. There is also a significant feud between two socialites--the lady who raises the funds for the orchestra and the lady who has started the festival and who thinks there are musicians who play only Bach.

The man in the middle of all this, Tony Farnum, is a rather unpleasant sort, with a penchant for blackmail. He is aware that his personal habits do not make him popular with most people and admits he would be a great candidate for murder. When he realizes that he has been poisoned and is about to die, he nonetheless is quite upset. You would have thought that he would have been pleased to discover his assessment was correct.

Two more deaths take place in the novel and one hit-and-run, the victim of the latter being a member of the symphony orchestra who seems to accuse Til Eulenspiegel, or, as the police would have it, Miss or Mrs. Tilly or Matilda Oylenshpiegel, and for whom they have instituted a city-wide search.

Not a classic, but a good, craftsman-like job, with a fair sprinkling of humor and insight into the thoughts, a word I use with some generosity, and spites of the upper classes. (William F. Deeck)

Alfred Eichler. *Death of an Ad Man*. Abelard-Schuman, 1954; Hammond, 1956, as *A Hearse for the Boss*; Berkley Books, no date, 128 pages.

It is a rather frantic time at the Malcolm and Reynolds Advertising Agency. Reynolds has retired, and Malcolm has just had what appears to be a heart attack. While various officials of the agency are struggling for power in an attempt to replace Malcolm as the agency's head, someone makes sure that Malcolm won't be around to protest. A pair of scissors is shoved into his chest while he is in the hospital.

Kindergarten was never like this advertising agency. Children do have some sense, but precious few employees of this agency have any. The only sensible person is Martin Ames--who appears in several of Eichler's novels--head of the radio department, which also includes television. Even he is erratic. He is at one point firmly convinced that an agency employee is Malcolm's murderer and a few moments later is brooding because he didn't stop the murderer from killing the employee.

Ames has inherited the agency from Malcolm, and he had an opportunity to commit both murders. For this reason, and in a hope to keep the agency from disintegrating, Ames investigates. He spots the killer by discovering a new motive for murder, or what would have been a new motive if it had had anything to do with the murder. He also says things like "Holy hatpin!" which I guess is typical advertising talk. And he is one of the few people who have visited a psychiatrist with a "crowded anteroom." Does this mean a ten-minute hour?

The novel isn't well written and the plot isn't that great, but the insights into advertising agencies may appeal to some. (William F. Deeck)

E.X. Ferrars. *Murder of a Suicide.* Doubleday, 1941; Hodder, 1941, as *Death in Botanist's Bay*; Curtis Books, no date, 192 pages.

Edgar Prees, director of the Botanical Gardens in Asslington, is a man of such regular habits that when he is two hours late coming home one evening his daughter becomes quite alarmed. And rightly so, for Prees has, or so it seems, tried to commit suicide by trying to throw himself off a cliff. He is stopped, but the next morning, even as he still seems to be thinking about killing himself, he is murdered. Or does he kill himself?

Officially, Inspector Tingey investigates. Tingey "liked simple virtues and was sympathetic to a few simple vices. He liked to be thought a simple man who believed what people told him." Unofficially, Toby Dyke and his rather odd companion George, of apparently fixed abode but no last name, both of whom had aided in keeping Prees from hurling himself off the cliff, try to help Prees's daughter, who is a possible suspect.

Most of the characters, with the possible exception of Prees's neurotic former secretary, are believable, including Gerald Hyland, an author who achieves a reasonable income by writing about "sex and religion in the desert" and who is the complete faddist.

There are wheels within wheels here. A plausible solution is offered at the end, and then it is overridden by an even more plausible solution.

For reasons that I cannot recall, I had thought that Ferrars was essentially a suspense writer. This, however, is a fair-play mystery. (William F. Deeck)

Gregory Dean. *Murder on Stilts.* Hillman-Curl, 1939; Detective Novel Classic No. 17, no date, 128 pages.

There are several things to be sought in a mystery novel. Style, to this reader, is foremost. When the author on page one writes, "He trajected his mind back," it is a pointer that style will not be found. Characterization comes next, and the author fails here, too. Finally—though to many readers the most important aspect of a book—comes plot.

In this area Dean gives good value for the money, particularly if you actually did pay a quarter for the reprint. A good, kindly, thoughtful rich man—most unusual in mystery novels—is murdered in a locked room. Although the murderer's intent was to have the man's death appear to be suicide, the murderer botched this aspect rather badly. The rich man was supposed to appear to have shot himself through his blanket while in bed, but there are no powder marks on the blanket. The window locks have been wiped clean of fingerprints, as has the safe in the room. Dirty work has obviously been afoot.

Fourth Deputy Commissioner Benjamin Simon is the investigator here. It is he who deduces murder rather than suicide. He also figures out early on how and who. He doesn't reveal it, thus being responsible for another murder. At the end of the novel when he finds out why, all is belatedly revealed.

Unfortunately, the explanation for the murder in the locked room, and a later appearance of the murderer there while the room again is locked and a policemen is in it, is rather lame. This novel will be of interest only to those who collect locked-room puzzles. It also may be of interest to another type of collector, but reviewers' rules do not allow that information to be divulged.

(If anyone is curious about the title, which is the only reason I bought the book, the murdered man lived in what was called "the house on stilts," a dwelling apparently constructed on a concrete arch. I say "apparently" because this is not mentioned in the novel; it is information provided by the paperback publisher.) (William F. Deeck)

Anthony Gilbert. *Death in the Blackout.* Smith & Durrell, 1943; Collins, 1942, as *The Case of the Tea-Cosy's Aunt*; Bantam Books No. 51, 1946, 249 pages.

It has been twenty years or so since I read an Arthur Crook novel by Anthony Gilbert, and those I had read had been from (I shall use the masculine gender to avoid confusion, though Gilbert was, of course, a female) his later period. The novels were supposed to be amusing, and I seldom found them so. Gilbert apparently did better in his earlier works.

Death in the Blackout is one of the early cases of Arthur Crook, lawyer. Whether Crook is a solicitor or a barrister, should anyone be curious, is information not provided by the author in this novel. Frankly, I don't recall his ever appearing in court; he seems to be primarily an investigator.

Crook's flat is in a building with several other occupants who are almost as strange as he is. A woman who sees spies in the most improbable disguises occupies the ground floor and basement, while flat No. 3 boasts the presence of T. Kersey, whom Crook immediately begins calling "Tea-Cosy" and who is a bit unsteady when it comes to the nature of time. Flat No. 2 is unoccupied.

Tea-Cosy asks Crook to help him check out his flat when he finds his key is missing. Therein he and Crook find a hat of a sort that could belong only to Tea-Cosy's aunt, but the aunt is not there. Later on, a young lady checking out the unoccupied flat in the hope of renting it discovers the aunt's body.

Tea-Cosy disappears before the body is found. Since Crook has adopted Tea-Cosy as a client, and Crook's clients are always not guilty even when they are, Crook begins investigating. Even when Tea-Cosy, or someone dressed to look like Tea-Cosy, nearly kills the young lady who comes back to the supposedly unoccupied apartment a second time, Crook knows that Tea-Cozy is innocent.

And, of course, Crook is right. Since there are only a few suspects, the guilty are rather evident, but it is quite interesting, and occasionally amusing, how Crook works it all out from the author's fair clues. (William F. Deeck)

Babette Hughes. *Murder in Church*. D. Appleton-Century, 1934, 234 pages.

Sir Arthur Quinn is a famous astrophysicist who is the bane of the religionists. He had shown "the theologians to be charlatans, religions to be apologies, and his more cautious confreres to be opportunists." Besides that, he is given to amorous intrigues, mushrooms for breakfast, and the sucking of fruit lozenges. It is the latter habit, possibly combined with the second, that brings about his death as he rather uncharacteristically attends Sunday services at St. Barnabas Church. Someone had coated several lozenges with muscarin, a poison that is derived from mushrooms.

Among the possibilities for the distinction of bumping him off are President Radford of the Western Institute of Technology, a pompous oaf who tries vainly to reconcile religion and science; Yozan Saijo, a Japanese physicist whom Quinn has insulted; Quinn's "sexless" wife who worships him despite his philandering; a professional dancer whose movements were harsh and whose interpretations were grotesque and often venomous, and who had been one of many of Quinn's inamoratas; George Coburn, Quinn's valet, an ex-English jockey who sports a black eye given him by Quinn; a fanatically religious Russian technician, and others too numerous to mention. Quinn had religious, scientific, and personal enemies, it seems.

Ian Craig, professor of Oriental literature at Stanford and frequent quoter of the aphorisms of Ti Li, is the amateur investigator. He gained some little renown when he solved the case chronicled in *Murder in the Zoo* (1932), another academic mystery.

One of the selections in "The Tired Business Man's Library," chosen to "afford relaxation and entertainment for everyone interested in Adventure and Detective Fiction," *Murder in Church* meets that goal, but only barely. (William F. Deeck)

Inigo Jones. *The Albatross Murders.* Arcadia House, 1941; The Mystery Novel of the Month, No. 33, 1941, 128 pages.

Inigo Jones, a pseudonym, wrote two mystery novels under that name: this one and *The Clue of the Hungry Corpse* (1939). The latter has nothing to recommend it, but *The Albatross Murders* I found quite enjoyable. Of course, that may be because I read it immediately after I read about the corpse who was peckish.

Somewhere in the Northeast, in a city that would have been a stop on the Underground Railroad, some young thespians are putting on a play. On opening night, an actor who is to be shot as part of the script is shot in reality, and the player shooting him—as part of the play or for real, deliberately or because someone gave him a loaded pistol by mistake or with malice aforethought—exits the stage and keeps on going out of the theater. An oddity in the killing is there is no bullet in the dead man and no exit wound.

Besides the gaggle of actors and actresses, the deceased's sister, who loathed him and is not very pleasant besides, was at the opening night and might have committed the murder, if only it could be figured out how the killing was accomplished if the actor who was supposed to have shot him as part of the play didn't do it and what became of the bullet. And what does the history of the area have to do with the murder? Nothing? Everything?

Sebastian Booth, State Police Inspector, solves the case and explains how the murder was done satisfactorily—even though it's as Rube Goldbergish a method as I have encountered in some time—in about twenty-four hours, but meanwhile three more people have died.

Booth is a delightful detective with a great deal of personality. He knows his mind and speaks it. In a case with many theater people, Booth says: "I'd as soon have a Gila monster around the house as an actress. Or an actor, either. I'll be glad when this case is broken. I long for the company of a simple-hearted thief or an honest hatchet murderer."

It is Booth's presence that makes *The Albatross Murders* a mystery worth reading. (William F. Deeck)

Rufus King. *Museum Piece No. 13.* Doubleday, 1946; Bantam Books, 1947, 150 pages, as *Secret Beyond the Door.*

Bantam Books describes this novel accurately as "suspense." A wealthy widow is cajoled into a frenzy or falls in love at first sight, or something like that, with a publishing tycoon, himself a widower. She apparently feels that he will be like her first husband, a dedicated coupon clipper who devoted himself to her. Her bankers, who cannot turn over her money to her unless she marries a suitable man—for which read "rich"—hurriedly give their imprimatur, though the tycoon would have been found to be in dire need of a fresh infusion of cash to keep his newspaper going if they had investigated a bit more thoroughly. She, with substantial wealth, would appear to have no lawyers to advise her.

After the whirlwind courtship--time not specified, but it probably was no more than a month, and possibly less--he marries her and leaves the next day on a business trip. (No information is given whether the marriage was consummated. I'd tend to think it wasn't.)

The tycoon collects rooms in which murders have taken place, buying them and moving them to his mansion intact, apparently even to the dust that was present at the time he bought them. Although the tycoon delights in giving tours of his collection, he does not allow a thirteenth room, recently finished, to be viewed by anyone.

It is obvious that the man is interested only in his new wife's money, and even she dimly begins to recognize this when she moves into his home with his strange sister, brother-in-law, secretary who wears a veil to cover a scar that doesn't exist, neurotic son, and a an egocentric star reporter.

Acting on advice of a psychiatrist who is making judgments on the woman's quite limited and mostly wrong knowledge of the tycoon and on almost no knowledge of the woman, the tycoon's new wife checks out room No. 13. Although her husband, when he's around at all, and the household are often out during the day, she needs must select 4 a.m. for her trip to the mysterious room.

King's writing style is sometimes convoluted: "Both parents having been of the old-fashioned school which brooked no trifling with the mathematical gymnastics of the marriage vows in adding one to one and getting one, with all the sum's attendant surfeiture of the unpictorial effects of contiguity and general minor inconveniences. Like when you wanted to read at night. Or when you didn't."

There are those who will master that at first reading. I am not one of them. But if you like that sort of thing, and I admittedly do, there's a fair amount of it here. (William F. Deeck)

Helen McCloy. *The One That Got Away.* Morrow, 1945; Gollancz, 1954; Dell Mapback No. 355, no date, 192 pages.

There may nor may not have been an escape by a German prisoner of war in Dalriada, Scotland. Lieutenant Peter Dunbar, a psychiatrist who is interested in youth delinquency, is assigned by his commanding officer, Basil Willing--also a psychiatrist and a continuing character in McCloy's novels--to find out if there was such an escape and where the German soldier might be hiding.

As soon as Dunbar arrives in the area, however, he becomes involved with the adopted son of a famous, albeit not much read, author and the author's tripe-writing but best-selling wife. The boy keeps trying to run away from home for reasons unknown. In the most recent episode, the boy, in full sight of a watcher, vanishes on the moor. He also pulls the same trick later, more or less. Dunbar, who was supposed to have been watching him, is busy ogling a young lady.

Dunbar's talents as a psychiatrist ought to be enhanced by his ability to read eyes. He knows when they have a twinkle in them, are wary and calculating, are full of tragedy. Since there are only two men in the area who could be the German escapee, if there is one, Dunbar's ability to read the messages in eyes ought to make his task easy. It doesn't. After two deaths, one in a locked-room-type situation, Basil Willing has to step in and clear up the case.

A good plot, some interesting characters, and enough misdirection to confuse both Dunbar and me. Perhaps if he hadn't fallen in love at first sight, he might have been able to do better. I didn't have that excuse. (William F. Deeck)

H.F.M. Prescott. *Dead and Not Buried*. Dodd, Mead, 1938; Constable, 1938; Collier Books, 1965, 191 pages.

There is no introduction to Old Marshall, the corpse. At the very beginning he has been brutally murdered. The man who did it is unknown to the reader, at least for a while. The woman who watches the murder being committed and who later shields the murderer is Marshall's wife.

Old Marshall's corpse disappears, so the police, in the form of Sergeant Tucker, a wise and thoughtful man no longer eager for success, don't know what has happened to Marshall. Did he just leave the farm or was there foul play?

On a nearby chicken farm live Mark (sometimes Marc) Yorke, monied, elegant, and a tad snobbish, and Philipson (first name unknown, which seems to happen frequently in mysteries, at least the ones I read), a shell-shocked sometime artist who is also quite clumsy, which saves his life on at least two occasions.

Despite the lack of a body, Philipson is suspected of having done away with Marshall. Unfortunately for Philipson, he is suffering from temporary amnesia about what happened the afternoon of Marshall's death.

The foregoing is a bare description that really does not do justice to this novel. The reader knows who did it fairly early on--a man who has murdered one person and has twice tried to kill another one, but who dog-ears a page in a book "with compunction.

Prescott has sketched her characters amazingly well, with attention to the small things that bring people alive. Most of them, particulary the vicar, the vicar's daughter, Sergeant Tucker, and Mrs. Harker, who cooks for Yorke and Philipson, are people you will enjoy having met.

Prescott wrote no other mystery novels, which is a great pity. Her talent was considerable.

For those who like their mystery novels catalogued, I would put this in the English-village and Holy Terror categories. (William F. Deeck)

The Documents in the Case

(Letters)

From Marvin Lachman, 34 Yorkshire Drive, Suffern, NY 10901:

I was glad to find out in advance, at Bouchercon, that TMF will continue. Regardless of whether you pay contributors or not, you know that old Marv Lachman will keep on sending you "It's About Crime" in Volume 10 and for as long thereafter as you publish. The money you paid was nice as a token and made me feel *semi*-professional, but I can understand your decision.

From Frank D. McSherry, Jr., 314 West Jackson, McAlester, OK 74501:

Current issue of *Mystery Fancier* ... quite a strong one, first two articles* and Lachman's column being especially powerful. Glad you're going on.
 *Worts' Gillian Hazeltine stories, biblio appreciated; Blom's on hard-boiled social protest writer Donald Goines, interesting look at how other countries may see us.

From Charles Shibuk, 2084 Bronx Park East, Bronx, NY 10462:

Alvin H. Lybeck will be interested to learn that George M. Cohan played the leading role in the 1932 film version of *The Phantom President.*
 I regret to say there are 3 cinematic errors in Marvin Lachman's necrological notes:
   1) The screenplay of *Laura* is credited to mystery writer Jay Dratler, Samnuel Hoffenstein, & Betty Reinhardt--not to Vera Caspary;
   2) *Chinatown* cannot be listed as a film that was either written or directed by John Huston. He did act in it, but *Chinatown* was directed by Roman Polanski & written by Robert Towne.
   3) Huston did not do the script for *Murders in the Rue Morgue.* Tom Reed and Del van Every did. Huston is credited with contributing additional dialogue to this film.

From William F. Deeck, 9020 Autoville Drive, College Park, MD 20740:

The news that TMF will continue through next year is satisfactory, indeed most satisfactory, which is the highest praise, as you will recall.

Yes, I know you weren't addressing me with your request for reviews, but unless you say "Bill Deeck need not apply," you can expect to get tome. I guarantee I read each one; I won't say that I always understand them.

Anyhow, it gives me the opportunity to explain, somewhat incoherently, why I flout the wise advice of Marv Lachman and others not to reveal too much plot in reviews. *Primo*, I don't have anything to say about a book usually unless I talk about plot, which any reader of my reviews has already noticed. *Secundo*, in almost all cases, the books I review are hard to find. Indeed, I or the Enoch Pratt Free Library in Baltimore, Md., may have the only copy still in existence. So if someone does locate a book I review, it will be long after the review, and doubtless he or she will not recall who reviewed it and what the review said. *Tertio* (and the last, because I don't know what the Latin is for fourth), I try, with limited or no success, to make the review enjoyable in itself since a lot of the books I read and review aren't worth looking for in my opinion.

K. Arne Blom's article about Donald Goines was fascinating. I shall have to try one of Goines's books, although it would not be my normal reading choice. On a side issue, as a provider to the Oxford English Dictionary of old and new proverbs, one of the suggested new proverbs is "what goes around comes around," which Mr. Blom quotes from Eddie Stone's biography of Goines. The 1974 use of the expression is eight years earlier than any I have discovered in print. I would certainly appreciate Mr. Blom's providing a publisher of Stone's book and the chapter and page number where the expression appears.

From Bob Sampson, 609 Holmes Ave., NE, Huntsville, AL 35801:

Loved the G. Hazeltine article in the new issue. I'll have to dig back among my scanty collection of *Argosy* but believe—at this point, only believe—that "Who Killed Ezra Klagg" was a Hazeltine. Will advise, whenever I get the lead out and check. [*Penned note in margin:* I did. See attached checklist w/corrections. Don't have enough Argosy to confirm all. *Bob's "checklist" is a photocopy of page 15 of TMF 9:4 with the following penned corrections: the Klagg story appeared in the 7 January 1928 issue; the correct year for "The Crime Circus" is 1928, not 1929; the correct date for the first appearance of "A Reptile Named Robard" is 21 September 1928; and the first appearance of "The Lost Punch" was 25 January 1930, not 26 January.*]

. . .

Hope that your new life among the law books gets more and more successful. It's the road to fame and wealth, no

The Documents in the Case (Letters)   49

denying. Some of the great men of our day have been lawyers—S. Agnew, for example. Or good old Ed Meese ...

   [*From another letter, inserted here in the hope that it will nudge Bob into sending TMF another article Real Soon Now. You are sorely missed, old horse.*] For two years, I've been carrying a note that I was to write something on ESG's White Rings for you. So I had better get off this pile of velvet cushions and get to work. The White Rings, in case you never ran into them, were a short-lived series featuring ESG's version of The Just Men. He did little with them. Interesting, isn't it, that The Just Men from the early 1900s were still influencing series thirty years later—although *Detective Story Magazine* had reprinted some of the short stories in the late 1920s. Both White Rings and The Park Ave. Hunt Society continue that admirable tradition, one of the more durable of the mystery-adventure lines.

From Ola Strøm, Postboks 2124, N-7001 Trondheim, NORWAY:

   Vol 9 no 3 with your editorial on the continuance of TMF with ensuing price increase really did arrive at a most awkward time, with the stock market sinking like the very Titanic and one wondering whether one is broke or is still going to see the light of another year.
   Well, from lottery to business. I acknowledge the sufferings of the spare time non-salaried editor and am prepared to accept any sensible course taken to keep the magazine alive.

Happy 20th Birthday, TAD!

Celebrate TAD's first two decades with this money-saving combination: a hardcover facsimile reprint of TAD's first volume and a trade paperback collection of eighteen essays and reminiscences on TAD's early days by founder Al Hubin and more than a dozen other luminaries who made it all happen. Both books—a $29.95 value—are available direct from Brownstone Books for $25.00 postpaid. Save $4.95 and treat yourself to hours of pleasurable reading in the company of TAD's leading lights:

The Armchair Detective, Volume One, smythe-sewn and bound in quality cloth, this facsimile reprint contains all 158 pages of the first four issues of TAD, plus a specially written Introduction by Allen J. Hubin; viii, 158 pp., available individually for $17.00 postpaid.

TAD-SCHRIFT: Twenty Years of Mystery Fandom in The Armchair Detective, edited by J. Randolph Cox, this quality trade paperback contains essays by Bob Adey, Jon L. Breen, Robert E. Briney, Joe R. Christopher, J. Randolph Cox, William K. Everson, John A. Hogan, Estelle Fox, Marvin Lachman, Edward S. Lauterbach, Frank D. McSherry, Jr., Francis M. Nevins, Jr., William F. Nolan, John Bennett Shaw, Charles Shibuk, Donald A. Yates, and a long survey of TAD's first decade by founder and long-time editor Allen J. Hubin; vii, 111 pp., available individually for $12.95 postpaid.

Also Available from Brownstone Books

Detective and Mystery Fiction: An International Bibliography of Secondary Sources, edited by Walter Albert, smythe-sewn and bound in quality cloth, this Edgar winner belongs on the reference shelf of every mystery fan worthy of the name; xii, 781 pp., $60.00 postpaid.

The Sound of Detection: Ellery Queen's Adventures in Radio, edited by Francis M. Nevins, Jr., and Ray Stanich, this illustrated, quality trade paperback, which consists of a detailed narrative history (by Nevins) of the long-running Ellery Queen radio program and an annotated log (by Stanich and Nevins) of the individual episodes, is a must for Queen fans as well as fans of Old Time Radio; viii, 109 pp., $6.95 postpaid.

The Mystery Fancier, second oldest generalist mystery fan publication in the United States (only TAD has been around longer), is now published quarterly in a trade-paperback format. A year's subscription is $25.00 (second class), $30.00 (first class in U.S. and Canada), or $35.00 (airmail overseas). Individual issues are $7.50 postpaid.

In the Brownstone Chapbook Series

Volume One: *Hardboiled Burlesque: Raymond Chandler's Comic Style*, by Keith Newlin, 50 pp., $4.95 postpaid.

Volume Two: *The New Hard-Boiled Dicks: A Personal Checklist*, by Robert E. Skinner, vii, 60 pp., $6.95 postpaid.

Volume Three: *John Nieminski: Somewhere a Roscoe*, selected and edited by Ely Liebow and Art Scott, 61 pp., $6.95 postpaid.

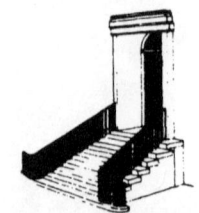

Brownstone Books
407 Jefferson Street
Madison, Indiana 47250
(812/265-2636)

www.ingramcontent.com/pod-product-compliance
Lightning Source LLC
Chambersburg PA
CBHW031435040426
42444CB00006B/825